SUPERCHARGE YOUR MOTIVATION AND PERFORMANCE

THE KEY TO ANYTHING YOU CAN IMAGINE THROUGH PLANNING, GRATITUDE, AND THE POWER OF YOUR MIND

By

MANOS FILIPPOU

2015

Thanks for support from

George Mabbutt, Bob Vaites, Brian McAulay and
Albert Korhonen

Reviewed by Andrew Vujnovich

In loving memory of Elmer Shehane, my Mom and Dad,
and my family's loving pets – Boo Boo and Trixie

Thanks to all who showed me unconditional love, helped me
believe in myself, made me understand I matter, and taught me to
never settle for less than I deserve.

SPECIAL THANKS

I have tried to acknowledge all the sources I have used or synthesized. I thank you for teaching me. Above all, thanks for letting me stand on your shoulders in my journey as I have tried to see my way forward. If I have missed someone, please tell me; it's not my intention or moral character to demean, or ignore value. And, if you care to add or improve to this offering, please let me know.

"… instructive, productive, upbeat, and hopeful, this book is a valuable addition to anyone's growth library …"

— George Mabbutt, Retired Businessman

CONTENTS

PROLOGUE

"Just imagine becoming the way you used to be as a very young child, before you understood the meaning of any word, before opinions took over your mind. The real you is loving, joyful, and free. The real you is just like a flower, just like the wind, just like the ocean, just like the sun." [1]

— Miguel Angel Ruiz, Mexican Author

There was a time of innocence where, as children, we saw possibility everywhere. We had no fear, no guilt; we did not know what limitation was. We truly believed we could become whoever we wanted to be and do whatever we wanted in our lives. We used our imagination and we created fantasy worlds where we could fly; we could swim for hours under water and we were the superheroes who saved our planet. How many times when we were children did each one of us save the world? Our only limitation was our imagination!

We dreamed big; we were unleashed. We didn't take "NO" for an answer. We were unstoppable. Our curiosity often got us in trouble as we excitedly explored new things and unknown territories. But, we didn't care. We had the freedom to express ourselves; we took action without much thinking. If we had the desire to play, we would do just that, without worrying about other people's expectations.

We made friends easily and even though sometimes we fought, the next moment we were best friends again, like nothing ever happened. Every day was a new adventure and we were constantly taking risks. Our creativity was wild. We used every possible item we could find as a prop to create our imaginary world, and we had everything we wanted. We had our family, our friends; we were happy, and our world was full of possibilities and adventure.

Then, as we grew older, we slowly, and without realizing it, started to limit ourselves. Like all things, the change started in our thoughts because in truth, that is the only place it ever happens. For many of us, limitations replaced possibilities; fear and guilt replaced fun and adventure. Surrounded by lack of imagination, unable to see new opportunities, we are constantly reminded by our new self, our environment, the media, and our society, what we are allowed and what we cannot do. We can't do this or that, because we have too little money, time, resources, and courage. We have an endless list of reasons why we can't do much of anything, and we become increasingly limited in our lives.

And, in those rare times that our inner child tries to come forward, we are immediately corrected by ourselves and others; "grow up", "act your age", "don't be foolish", "this will never happen", "stop dreaming, you are not a child any more", "you are too old to do this".

What an amazing story we could tell one day, if we just started ignoring those limitations and rediscovered ourselves and who we really are. What if, instead of seeing limitation everywhere, we see possibilities, and we use our imagination and experiences to build and live our life exactly the way we want it, and as the true miracle we are and life is.

We have only one life to live, and there is no guarantee of tomorrow. We need to make every day count and go after what we truly want in life and those things that inspire us. We have to find again the innocent self of our childhood; look in the mirror and ask "What do you, really, really want?" Then, when we receive our answer, we have to go after it and be committed 100%. No reasons, no excuses, no guilt, no regrets! We may not know at that moment how we will accomplish what we want, but we will find our way. Everything starts with your decision to change. This book gives you the tools and the motivation you need to go after your true passions and goals, **if only you choose to do it**. [2]

INTRODUCTION

A MESSAGE FROM MANOS

I truly believe each one of us has enormous potential. Absolutely anything we can imagine and want in life, we can have. The only things that may stop us from getting what we really want are the thoughts we have in our minds, the way we view life, and the way we view ourselves as a possibility.

My intention is to genuinely share, without hesitation, personal opinions, ideas and beliefs, knowledge and experiences, and tested tools and techniques that may inspire readers to go after whatever goal they want in life and to accomplish it. My ultimate goal is to have a positive impact on others, and help people realize what they may think is impossible, in the end IS possible, and closer to their reach than they may think.

What a better example than this book?

When I first started writing this book, I often laughed because I knew I'm an immigrant from Greece living in Canada, with a strange accent (even though some people really like it), and speaking what I often call "broken English" – yet, I had the nerve to dare to write a book about motivation. This is living proof you can wake up one day with an "idea" – which in this case is to write a book – and be able to face your own fears, negative thoughts, and all the other obstacles that tell you it is impossible. I gave myself many negative thoughts and the excuses to not move forward and write this book. Here are some examples: "I do not have an excellent command of the English language – people will make fun of me", "I do not have the experience of writing a book. I do not know what writing a book involves, I have no idea what to write and I'm not sure how I will do it", "I'm not an expert, most likely others know many more things than I do", "I do not have the time and I'm very busy to do this". Let's not forget the opinions of others, who initially gave fuel to those negative thoughts.

It takes a Herculean effort to fight everything in your environment, including yourself, telling you "you can't", to actually make the decision and go after what you want, and to thrive in your own way, no matter the circumstances and obstacles you face. When you take action, you gain the determination needed, you believe in yourself, and you become open to the idea you may have to figure things out as you go; then, anything is absolutely possible. This book is completed because I made the conscious decision I would finish, no matter what, and I did it. I know you can do exactly the same, if you set a goal and focus on it.

I understand things may often not be as easy, and you may have valid reasons to believe you cannot have what you want. I used to have those reasons and excuses as well, and my personal "stories" and what I thought "misfortunes" often prevented me from reaching my goals and ultimately excellence.

When I was growing up I had every reason to accept failure, give up, and ultimately fail in life. I lost my father to cancer when I was only nine. My mother had serious health problems most of her life – what the doctors diagnosed as schizophrenia – unable to always take care of herself or me. It is interesting because even just writing the word "schizophrenia" makes me feel uneasy, but at the end that's what it was. I knew I had a mother who really loved me, she was very smart when she was healthy; but when she had her relapses, things were not always easy. For many years we lived way below the poverty line; I always worried how we were going to make it to the next day. My mother used to tell me when I was 9 years old I was only 9 kilograms. I was very frail, I was getting sick all the time, and I think I was what we call today anorexic. I didn't really like or enjoy food, but it is possible a lot had to do with the fact we didn't have much food around anyways. Bread with sugar, spaghetti with tomatoes and cheese, and homemade potatoes are the things I remember the most.

During my teenage years and early adult life, I was a skinny, short, young man, constantly rejected by the opposite sex. And when I got old enough to figure out my true sexual orientation, I came to understand I was living in a society who would never accept who I was. I was gay and I found much older chubby men attractive. I'm not sure what was more challenging – living in a Greek society then who did not accept gay people, a society that made fun of the desire to want to be with a much bigger person, or the gay community believing if you like older men, you want them only for their money and you are a gold-digger.

As an entrepreneur, I worked 80-plus hours a week for many months, only to see my business plans fail, while putting myself into serious financially trouble. Nevertheless, I wanted desperately to accomplish my dreams and I was willing to take all the necessary risks. Very often I questioned my choices and what I was doing. I think the hardest thing of all was the criticism of others. I often heard the comment "why don't you get a job?" But, I had a job!! I didn't make money, but I had a job working harder than anyone else I knew of, while I was putting everything on the line, sacrificing so many things, including not spending time with my family and the people I loved.

I can share many more "stories" about my "difficulties", my reasons, and my excuses why things were not working out. The fact though is in every situation the defining common factor was me. It was me who didn't always have confidence; I was letting the negative thoughts take over. It was me who always compared myself to others and I felt I was a failure. It was me who thought that other people were smarter, had more knowledge, and were luckier than I was, and it was me who was afraid to stand up for myself when I had every reason to fight. In every situation it was me! I felt sorry for myself countless times; I was building my own reality based on my own perception of the world. Bottom-line, it was no one else but me who was holding me back for so many years.

My biggest mistake over all these years was I was so intensely focused on my "failures" and misfortunes; I simply didn't acknowledge all the amazing things I had, or I had accomplished, despite the circumstances and the difficulties I had in life. I had the best mother in the world – at times she acted strange due to her illness – but she would do anything to protect me and she offered unconditional love. I always knew I was loved. I'm the one who didn't always appreciate her love, her advice, and how smart she really was. The rest of my immediate family, my sisters, were always there for me in the best way they could – I just couldn't see it. I found a genuine person who fulfilled the emptiness I felt for so many years of not having a father figure in life, and now I call my dad. I always had the best friends – people who had my best interests in their hearts. My childhood was not actually as traumatic as I thought, but absolutely outstanding with a lot of laugher and fun. I was the first person from my extended family getting a university degree in a department that was very difficult to get into. As a gay man, I went into the army for a year and not only did I survive, but I proved to myself I was tougher than I thought. I moved to a new country, Canada, I learned a new language, and over time I traveled to more than a dozen countries accumulating experiences and meeting some very interesting people. Through discipline, I beat my anorexia; with hard work and training, I built a healthy and strong body. I have a happy family life, a successful career, and I accomplished most of the things I wanted to do. I'm looking with excitement to the future, because I know that more amazing things are going to happen.

Sometimes it feels like a dream how far I have come. Despite the fact the odds were not really on my side, despite the fact I had some very difficult times and suicide seemed at times the only option, now I can look back and genuinely appreciate all these experiences. I would have never been the person I am today if my past was different. And I would have never been able to motivate other people, without being able to empathize, understand what they may be going through, and truly believe they can change their circumstances and have an absolutely amazing life.

I believe, without a single doubt, every person has the potential to live an outstanding life, and accomplish any goal, no matter how big or small that goal may be. There is nothing stopping you except you! Be true to who you really are, and what you really want. Without fear, take the risk, stand up for yourself and what you believe; go after what you want with respect, integrity, and dignity, while you generously share yourself with others. When you are genuine and you do not have a hidden agenda, people will eagerly open up, share their thoughts and goals with you, and help you towards what you want to accomplish.

The world really is your oyster. Decide what you really want in life, and then full speed, go for it!

CHAPTER 1

WHO SHOULD READ THIS BOOK AND HOW

"The question isn't who is going to let me; it's who is going to stop me." [1]

— Ayn Rand, Russian-American Novelist

Have you ever thought about why or even how some people accomplish more than others? What is it that makes some people high achievers, while you may be struggling to accomplish even the smallest goal?

This book answers these questions and provides ideas, concepts, and tools to everyone who wants to motivate him/herself or their loved ones, and who chooses to go after what he/she really want in life. It is written for two categories of people:

1. People who have specific goals (small or big); they know exactly what they want to accomplish, but they do not have the motivation to either start, continue, or finish what they have started.

2. People who do not have a specific goal, life plan, or know what they want, but they dream of a better, improved life

and are willing to try different approaches to make this possible.

As most of us belong to one category or other – sometimes both, it is safe to assume the concepts of this book apply to almost everyone. It may even help a large mass of non-believers, nay-sayers who pooh-pooh motivational sciences and holistic approaches. I am not pushing them; I welcome them with open arms to a world and life of amazing possibilities, if and when they choose to believe.

Of course, this book is not the magic pill – the silver bullet – that solves every problem or answers every question. You should not expect just by reading the book, things will start happening. You need to decide to take action and work to apply the concepts and ideas on a daily basis. You may find some ideas are completely new to you, and some others are concepts you already know and have tried, just presented from a different point of view.

There is not a rule-of-thumb. Focus on the ideas and concepts that make sense to you and you would like to try. You can start reading the book from the very beginning, or simply read the table of contents and jump to the chapters you think will benefit you the most. Personally, when I read self-help books, I first read the chapters I find interesting and intriguing, and then I read the whole book just in case I missed something important.

Before you continue reading the rest of the book, and to put things in perspective, I recommend doing the following:

1. Devote some time to think of the things you really want at this moment in life – after all this is the reason you are

reading this book – to get motivated and go after these things. Record them – journal, calendar, computer – just do it!

What do you want most in life? Is it money, career, fame, power, contentment, personality, peace of mind, happiness? Do you want to lose weight? Is your goal to start going to the gym or is it to find a partner? Whatever those goals may be, small or big, record them. Next to each goal, indicate how important it is to you by choosing a number from a scale of 1 to 10 where1 is the least important goal and 10 the most important goal.

2.   The next step is to spend some time and imagine you have achieved your goals again. How would that feel? Record those emotions, also.

3.   The third step is to record the things, or reasons you think are stopping you from having accomplished each one of your goals. Some of those reasons may be valid, but some may just be excuses you give to yourself for not having accomplished your goals. Just be honest with yourself and record those reasons or excuses. This is your record for your use, unless you share.

4.   Record how you presently feel about not having accomplished your goals.

Some other questions you may want to consider answering are:

•   What is that moves, touches, and inspires you in life?

•   What are you eager to give up or do to accomplish

what you want?

- What is the deadline you are giving yourself to accomplish your goal?

- If right now you could choose one goal only, which would it be? What helps you decide is the number (1 to 10) you assigned in step 2.

- Are you willing to temporarily give up other goals to focus completely on #1?

- Ask yourself if that goal is real; it is what you really want, and it is not affected by what others expect of you.

Keep a list of the things you want to accomplish, save all your answers and record the date. Once you read the book, I would be interested to know what things you have accomplished within a 3-month period, whether my book helped you at all, or what else you got out of reading it. You are welcome to email me your feedback at: manos_25@hotmail.com. And, I thank you!

In this book, we will explore how the mind works, what stops us from achieving our goals, and what are the steps we can take to get what we want. It is written based on my own experiences, my own training on personal development, my beliefs, and how I view life. In addition, it is based on research including reading books, watching online videos, reading articles, and following the brilliant work of others. In a nutshell, this book is my own interpretation of everything I know and understand about motivation, and what makes sense to me.

Don't be afraid to share your thoughts while you read this book, and solicit the point of view of friends, family members, colleagues, or any other people important to you who you know are objective and can act as observers. Discuss with them your goals, but also the ideas and concepts of this book. Their feedback can become really valuable and give you the additional inspiration you may need to move forward. Don't be afraid to seek inspiration from anyone else you think can help you reach your goals. Become a sponge of knowledge, and keep reading and expanding your knowledge and your level of awareness.

CHAPTER 2

UNDERSTANDING YOUR MIND

"The world we have created is a product of our thinking; it cannot be changed without changing our thinking." [1]

– Albert Einstein, Theoretical Physicist

Understanding the power of mind

The mind is very powerful; it is the beginning of anything we want to accomplish. Everything we do, we do in our minds first. The right mindset can set you apart from others and help you accomplish your goals, while the wrong images and "voices" in your head may prevent you from moving forward, giving you "valid" reasons to stop. Your mind may often play games and tell you that you CAN NOT do this and that, providing reasons that seem real and making decisions on your behalf, when you actually CAN accomplish anything you want. The reality you live is based on your beliefs and thoughts you have in your mind. Changing your beliefs and thinking, you are able to change your reality. Understanding the power of your mind and how it really works, helps you control it; ultimately you will be able to guide your mind in the direction you want, to achieve your goals.

What is the mind?

Although there is a misconception by many people that the brain is our mind, the mind is actually the element of people that enables them to be aware of the world and their experiences, to think, and to feel. The mind is the faculty of consciousness and thought, a switching system that operates part of our brain.

How does the mind work?

To understand how our mind works, we need to consider:

1. We think in pictures

2. The mind is divided into the conscious mind and the subconscious mind

We think in pictures!

An important element of the thinking process is the use of "images". We think in pictures; when there is no picture in our mind, there is confusion and no direction. Since we do everything in our minds first, when we bring pictures in, we organize our thoughts, we bring clarity to our mind, and an understanding of what needs to be done next. That's why visualization is so vital in many endeavors like sports, Olympics, music, personal development, and optimal performance.

The first and most important step to understand how our mind works, how we organize our thoughts, is to acknowledge we think in images, and encourage ourselves to develop this skill by practicing constantly. Experiment, and put yourself in various scenarios where you choose your thoughts. Think in images seeing exactly what you want in every possible detail. If, for example, you want to buy a new car, imagine going to the dealership. Think in images what you are wearing, how does the dealership look, imagine seeing your dream car, how you feel, and finally, imagine yourself at the desk in front of the sales person signing the agreement and buying that dream car. When we use our imagination and we consciously practice thinking in images, we form a new reality.

The mind is divided into the conscious mind and the subconscious mind

Literature uses different terms to define the conscious mind, the subconscious mind, and what are the differences. Even experts in psychology struggle defining the terms; often, mistakenly, they are used interchangeably. For the purpose of this book, for simplicity, and to understand how the mind works, we will make and accept the hypothesis the mind is divided into two systems: The conscious mind and the subconscious mind.

Conscious mind is the intellectual thinking mind. This is the part of you with the ability to think. We have the ability to choose to accept or reject in our conscious mind. Unfortunately we have the tendency to live through our senses and to react to what we hear, see, smell, taste, and touch, and we do not think. We use our senses to pick up information from the outside world and we let people and situations control us, instead of letting our mind think and make our own decisions. If, for example, someone tells us we are not good enough at something, we may accept that information as a fact and extend it on a larger scale – we are not good at anything! The reality is, that comment at a specific moment, has nothing to do with our ability to move forward.

While we have the ability to think, to use our mind, and to make plans to go ahead, we often do not do that. Most of us react only to situations around us, and then we wonder why things do not go our own way.

We are shaped by our thoughts, and we become what we think about. Start trusting the power of your conscious mind and your ability to think anything you want with clarity and in the most constructive way that will benefit you in the long run. That is the only way to move forward. While you do that, use tools and techniques to enhance your thinking ability. You may want to try techniques that will help you improve your memory, or you may want to use your imagination to create new ideas. Make sure you always track those ideas by recording them. In conclusion, let the will to accomplish your goals lead you. Remember, even though people see things from a different point of view, in the end what matters is what works for your situation. While you move forward, be present and aware of what is around you, and trust your intuition.

Subconscious mind is your emotional mind, and is controlled by the thoughts you entertain. The subconscious mind has no ability to think, choose or reject, and cannot differentiate between thoughts which are real or just imagined – it can only accept and, will, accept anything. To put this into perspective, think of babies as they accept any information randomly coming from their environment.

Whatever we put in the subconscious mind will be expressed via our body through feelings and in the form of action or non-action. As Henry Ford said, "Whether you think you can, or you think you can't – you're right." If you think you can do something, then you will take the necessary actions. If you think you can't, then you will do nothing about it.

How does the mind work – What is the process?

Simply, our thoughts create our reality. Our mind is divided into conscious thinking mind and subconscious emotional mind. We chose our thoughts and think in pictures. We then impress those images, thoughts, suggestions from our thinking mind to the emotional mind by autosuggestion, which is just repetition of thoughts and affirmations. We impress thoughts upon the subconscious mind and that causes us to feel the way we feel. The body then moves to action (or non-action), and our actions produce results. The mistake the most people make is trying to change the results instead of monitoring what they think. The results are something outside of us and something we cannot always control.

Start monitoring your thinking

It is crucial to start monitoring your thoughts – what you are thinking about. Most people think about what is going on around them, instead of the things they want to accomplish. There is a difference between being aware of your environment and being present and living your life through the lives of others and letting "what is happening" in your environment consume you. Constantly following celebrity news is an example of unproductively using your mind power.

Once you identify your goal and what you want to accomplish, start monitoring your own thinking constantly. Replace any negative thoughts with powerful positive thoughts, and any thoughts that take you away from your goal, to thoughts that take you closer. Think more of the things that make you happy and grateful, rather than the things that make you frustrated and unhappy. This is the miracle of positive thinking.

In addition, devote five minutes each night to record what has happened during the day. Remember the situations you had to deal with during the day and how you felt. Record anything negative you discover about yourself during the day and what you would do the next day to change those negative responses.

As you move forward, you need to constantly remind yourself you are able to accomplish anything you put your mind to, no matter how difficult it may seem. If you conceive an idea, then you can make it happen.

Often you may find you are unable to make a decision, you doubt your thoughts, and you are in fear. Indecision, doubt, and fear are the three enemies of the mind. Indecision is the seedling of fear. Indecision crystalizes into doubt, then the two blend together and become fear. While you monitor your thoughts, you need to identify these three enemies of the mind and eliminate them to move forward. [2]

Adopt a practice of making initially quick decisions on unimportant things (example: what you are having for dinner), until you gain confidence to make decisions on more important matters. Trust your instinct when there is a doubt; while you practice on a daily basis, challenge yourself to face things you fear.

By understanding, constantly monitoring our mind, and eliminating from our mind indecision, doubt, and fear, we can make anything we want happen.

CHAPTER 3

OUR BELIEF SYSTEM AND PARADIGMS

*"Beliefs have the power to create and the power to
destroy. Human beings have the awesome ability to take
any experience of their lives and create a meaning that
disempowers them or one that can literally save their lives."* [1]

– Anthony Robbins, American Motivational
Speaker and Writer

Two things control just about everything in your life and create your reality. Your beliefs and paradigms control your logic, perception of situations, what you think is possible, your happiness and success, and pretty much everything else.

What is a belief?

A belief is an acceptance that a statement is true, or something exists, and it is how we have come to view the world.

A *"belief system"* is a *set* of mutually supportive *beliefs* in a community or society as something one accepts as **true or real** and firmly holds an opinion or conviction. Your belief system is the actual set of precepts from which you live your daily life, those which govern your thoughts, words, and actions. Your deep emotions, likes, dislikes opinions and fears are all governed by your beliefs.

Centuries ago, we believed the world was flat. Common belief in ancient Greece was totally different from what it is today. And, in another 2000 years, it will likely be completely different again. Common belief is not necessarily true or accurate; believing something about life, doesn't make life that way. Believing the world is flat, even if all do, does not make it real. Believing negative things such as, you will always be poor, things will never change, life is a struggle and you will die alone, are nothing more than statements and beliefs, not true or real.

Your belief-system and paradigms are your "auto-pilot" – the beliefs you hold and the facts you take for granted are what causes you to think and feel the way you do. Your belief-system will determine your courage, fears, and behaviors, and whether you're depressed, happy, sad, or excited. Beliefs you hold about yourself and your environment are the root of all your wonderful and negative experiences in your life and determine how successful you will become.

You only need to examine your life to see your belief-system at work, as reflected in your level of success, your health, wellbeing, and quality of your relationships.

What cultivates our belief system?

We develop our beliefs by using our environment as a foundation we build upon. The belief system starts affecting us when we are kids and controls our future. The people we spend most of our time with, our parents, our friends, where we live, our school, our religion, our country, and the many forms of media we consume are examples of what cultivates our belief system. From the moment we enter this life, our subconscious mind collects and processes information. Combined with our experiences, this information is used to create our beliefs about who we are and how we fit into the world around us.

Beliefs may differ in different periods of time, and from society to society. People had different beliefs 200 years ago than they do now, and people born in societies with strict social rules and behavioral etiquette, have different beliefs from people born in societies that are less strict and more open-minded.

Often very successful people are born in environments that do not believe you "can be", "can do", and "can have". Their environment is not supportive because mediocrity and doing things the "normal/standard way" is all they know; they do not think IT IS possible. People in our life are affected (learn) by previous generations and beliefs continue from generation to generation, unless someone decides to change them. Successful people are eager to take a step forward, take risks, and upgrade the beliefs that do not serve them anymore.

What is a paradigm?

Paradigm comes from the Greek παράδειγμα (paradeigma), meaning "pattern, example, sample". A paradigm is a collection of very deeply ingrained ideas formed slowly over time, and controls our behavior and ultimately our life.

We get into the habit of doing things by repetition. Any idea that goes repetitively into our subconscious mind becomes fixed. Fixed ideas are commonly known as habits and a multitude of habits are called paradigms. A paradigm is a framework, guided by other people's habits, ways of thinking, prejudices, and limitations. A paradigm ultimately is our perception of reality, our view of the world. It is our interpretation of events based on previous teaching we have received. **Those teachings and experiences shape our belief system.**

Paradigms are lodged so deep in our subconscious mind we are rarely ever conscious of what they are. Yet not knowing about them doesn't negate they're in effect all day, every day. They form our auto-pilot that gets us through the day – They are the *what* we believe and *why* we believe it.

Paradigms are developed very gradually, usually at a very young age, require *a lot* of repetition of the same information to properly form, and are not easy to change. Our minds are wide open between the ages 0-5 and since we are not old enough to think for ourselves, our paradigms are formed for us, by those closest to us in those years – ultimately for better or worse.

And thus, by the time we can think for ourselves, we're going to think and act in accordance to the already-formed paradigms. [2]

Ideas repeated constantly by someone at an early age stick with you throughout the years. "You are not good enough", "you will never succeed", "your family is the only one who cares for you", "we are not Rockefellers to buy that" are examples of ideas that can become paradigms.

If we ask ourselves questions like "what was I doing when I was little", "what was the environment I was raised in", "what did I learn about love, work ethic, values, etc. from my family", we can see what is programmed into our subconscious.

Beliefs and Paradigms need to be upgraded

Understanding the mind is only **creative,** helps us grasp the power of beliefs. [3]

Our perception of reality is heavily influenced by our beliefs and paradigms. Because the process is happening on a subconscious level, we do not realize we create our own reality. If, for example, we believe life is only challenges and misfortunes, then this becomes our reality and we do not see any opportunities even if these are in front of us. Our awareness level is limited and we are unable to see what is obvious and makes sense. Other people with higher awareness levels and other beliefs will be able to identify those opportunities.

To grow and move forward, we need to re-examine and, if necessary, upgrade our beliefs – yes, upgrading beliefs and paradigms is possible as long as we are willing to do the change and we are willing to put in the necessary effort. The process starts by identifying our current beliefs and figuring out which ones need upgrading. **Since beliefs and paradigms are what limit us, they need to be changed to change our life to the life we want.**

How do we know though what beliefs and paradigms we need to re-examine and change? **Well, we need to look at the results.**

From the position you are in life today, judging by how you think and feel about yourself, you instinctively know whether your current beliefs are benefiting you, or simply holding you back. **You need to consider what works and what doesn't. What are those areas of your life where everything works great and what are those areas in your life where things are not going that well?** Record those areas. Any area in life where we are producing good results is probably anchored to an empowering belief and paradigm. Likewise, any area in our life plagued with unsatisfactory or frustrating results is likely anchored to a limiting belief and paradigm. A massive shortcut to the process of finding and replacing beliefs is using the experience and beliefs of others to test your own. The beliefs you don't like, you do not want to try but the ones that make you feel uncomfortable, are the beliefs you need to test the most.

Look for empowering replacements

After finding the beliefs and paradigms we need to upgrade, the next step is to look for empowering replacements. What are the paradigms and beliefs that will motivate you and inspire you? Those are the beliefs and paradigms you need to replace. If you do not know how to find those powerful replacements, think who you want to become, and who are the people you admire and who inspire you. If you admire people with great leadership skills, self-confidence, and charisma, then those are the new paradigms and beliefs you want to instill. **When we replace self-doubt with self-confidence, fear with curiosity, or pessimism with optimism, then, based on the new beliefs, our reality and the way we view the world will change. The world around us will look and feel different, and we will be more comfortable with our place in it.** [4] Adopting these new empowering beliefs will change the results you produce. In turn, being alert to those changes will help reinforce and validate your new beliefs. Soon, your new beliefs will be totally accepted into your subconscious mind.

How do we upgrade our beliefs and paradigms? – To change your life you need to decide to change your life.

"It's the repetition of affirmations that leads to belief. And once that belief becomes a deep conviction, things begin to happen." [5]

– Muhammad Ali, American Former Professional Boxer

We are programmed to do things the way we do by paradigms and beliefs; we are limited by other people's way of thinking, prejudices, and limitations. It is our obligation to change that to become optimal. As we try to move forward and grow, the old paradigms and beliefs kick in and hold us back. While our thoughts are going to the subconscious mind and tell us "I will change", paradigms dictate what we are going to do, and give us "valid" reasons why we cannot do what we want. This is because our thoughts and behaviors are largely controlled by the old paradigm. Paradigms influence our thinking and influence what we do. We can repeat a lot of stuff, but the paradigm still controls our behavior.

When we try to enforce new paradigms and beliefs there will be an internal fight. At the end, what will determine which one will win – the old VS new – is the GOAL we want to accomplish. Our goal should be really big and something we want, with every inch of our existence, to influence, and in the end change the old paradigms and beliefs.

While it may not seem easy at the beginning, WE ARE capable of changing the old paradigms and beliefs and choosing whatever we want to do, and become whoever we want to be. Period!

How do we do that?

In a nutshell, as we become what we think about – and we think in images – the first step is to build an image in our mind (conscious mind) of what we want to do or who we want to become. The second step is to embed that image into our subconscious mind and keep on programming it into our mind by repetition, until we start doing it. Repetition is extremely important. One tiny step repeated again and again, may produce huge results and bring big changes. We have to believe the change will happen, and we have to acknowledge it when it happens. As we may have more than one paradigm or belief we want to change, we have to take our time and focus on changing one paradigm or belief at a time and allow it to enter our life. Then we move to the next one.

To Change Your Belief System

We change our belief system by changing our subconscious mind. Here are the steps you can follow to change your beliefs and eventually change your life:

1. **Acknowledgment and Understanding:** The purpose of this chapter is to share knowledge and help you understand how beliefs and paradigms affect our life and behaviors. Until we understand and acknowledge their effect, we are not going to be able to make changes. Read this chapter again and do more research if you need clarity; be prepared to spend the time and energy

needed and do the necessary work required to achieve the results you want.

2. **Desire:** All changes to our belief system happen at the subconscious level, for those changes to stay in place. We can ultimately break down old paradigms holding us back through a desire to change. Our desire has to be strong enough to support us and withhold when the old paradigms challenge us. You must want that something, and you must want it badly enough.

3. **Strong feelings:** Getting emotionally connected with our desire is crucial. You must generate passion or intense emotion about having the desire.

4. **Decision:** Start with the decision that will change your belief system from a limiting one holding you back to an empowering one helping you move forward. Stand by your decision no matter what obstacles you may face. You should not procrastinate; you must act on that decision right away.

5. **Clear image of your goal:** You need to have a clear image of your goal and what you want. There shouldn't be any confusion or uncertainty. The goal has to be so big it will motivate you and inspire you. Create a very specific goal and record it. By doing that you materialize a thought; you give your goal an actual existence. Once you've thought of your goal and have written it, say it out loud and repeat it to yourself, not once or twice a day but 100-200 times.

6. **Monitor your thinking and the information you digest:** You need to start monitoring your thinking and exclude anything negative and not in agreement or alignment with your goal. We live in a world where thoughts and images of lack and limitation are everywhere. For that reason, being conscious of the thoughts you let into your mind is extremely important. In addition, you need to monitor the information you digest. Listen to audio, read books, connect with people, and watch things that will nourish and strengthen the new ideas.

7. Repeat, repeat, repeat! **Your deep subconscious mind is the very place where change happens:** You must repeatedly impress your conscious and subconscious minds with the new thoughts, images, affirmations, and the strong feelings that accompanied them, until this repetition changes your belief system or paradigm.

   Repetition is the secret to developing a powerful belief and you need to create and establish those new pathways that will have lasting results. It requires the discipline of repetition to change your deepest thoughts and beliefs about the nature of the world – and that is exactly what you must do to change your limiting beliefs that hold your back. [6]

   Habits are made and broken in a span of 21 to 30 days, as a rule. Repeating a set of effective affirmations three times each day for each habit, begins to create a new path in your brain. Repetition for 21 to 30 days can greatly increase the odds of making permanent change.

When you start repeating a set of affirmations, it will feel uncomfortable in the beginning. The old habits will kick in, and they will try to take over. You need to consider it takes time to get over the comfort hump and you need to be persistent. Set that time limit before you begin. Never, ever set it after. Stick to it and don't quit.

Your paradigms CAN be changed, and you can do it a little bit each day through repetition. [7]

8. **Consistency:** You must be persistent. Changes will happen through daily increases of awareness, time, and a lot of patience! You must REPEATEDLY impress the new images onto the subconscious mind until it manifests through the change in your belief system or paradigm.

CHAPTER 4

CREATIVE PROCESS

"The will to win, the desire to succeed, the urge to reach your full potential... these are the keys that will unlock the door to personal excellence." [1]

– Confucius, Chinese Teacher, Editor, Politician, and Philosopher

"One of the strangest things is the act of creation. You are faced with a blank slate—a page, a canvas, a block of stone or wood, a silent musical instrument. You then look inside yourself. You pull and tug and squeeze and fish around for slippery raw shapeless things that swim like fish made of cloud vapor and fill you with living clamor. You latch onto something. And you bring it forth out of your head like Zeus giving birth to Athena. And as it comes out, it takes shape and tangible form. It drips on the canvas, and slides through your pen, it springs forth and resonates into the musical strings, and slips along the edge of the sculptor's tool onto the surface of the wood or marble. You have given it cohesion. You have brought forth something ordered and beautiful out of nothing. You have glimpsed the divine." [2]

– Vera Nazarian, The Perpetual Calendar of Inspiration

Creative Process

To understand the creative process, we are going to divide our thoughts into two categories, depending on our awareness level and understanding of what we want, and the level of depth we have to go into our minds to find our answers.

1. We have a vague idea of what we want, but haven't figured out specifics. A vague idea may be akin to the context of "I do not look good in this dress. I want to look better in my clothes" or "someday I want to have a lot of money". Vague ideas are difficult to follow through and usually do not take us far. We think about them, but usually we do not do anything about them.

   In the contrary, a specific idea may be "I want to lose 30 pounds within 4 months", or "I want to have my first million by the age of 30". These types of goals are easier to accomplish. During the creation process, we need to turn these vague ideas, into specific ones.

2. We have the burning desire TO BE and TO DO, but we do not know how this will look like, and we haven't figured out what we need to do next. This is where we need to explore really deep in our minds to find our answers.

Regardless if we want TO BE and TO DO and we do not know how, or we have a vague idea and we are trying to clarify the specifics in our minds, the creative process is the same.

"A Burning Desire To Be and To Do is the starting point from which the dreamer must take off. Dreams are not born of indifference, laziness or lack of ambition." [3]

– Napoleon Hill, Personal Success Author

The two steps of the creative process

These are the main two steps of the creative process:

1. Step 1: Figure out what you really want.

2. Step 2: Focus on your goal; do not allow present results to influence you.

STEP 1 of two

The first and most important step of the creative process is to figure out exactly what you really want and desire.

This is the time to use your imagination and allow your inner child to come out.

This is your greatest opportunity to create something out of nothing and become, do, and accomplish whatever you want. The creative process starts by putting to the side of your mind what you already know, and starting fresh by writing down ideas that come to your mind. You may want to meditate or engage in mindfulness practice before you start recording your ideas. When you are at ease, you have juices flowing and this is where you become very creative. This is called creation. If you do not have a plan or know what you want, ask what will touch move, and inspire you, and help you see yourself as a possibility.

Think of your life as a blank canvas. This is yours to create from the very beginning – whatever you want. Record anything that comes into your mind even though it may not make sense at the moment. Keep on recording for a maximum of ten minutes and do not stop, even though you may think there is nothing to say. Use and trust your intuition, and allow your imagination to take you to places you have never been before. Dream like when you were a kid, and remember there is abundance (as in nature) and opportunity is everywhere. Dream big! Ideas are born in our conscious thinking mind, so think and allow the ideas to flow. For the imagination to work effectively, we need to fantasize and focus NOT on what we know we can do or we think we can do **but what actually inspires us.** Record your answers to: What is it you really want? What is it you really desire, what keeps you awake at night, and you're afraid to tell others because they will not understand? Record this.

Spend a maximum of 10 minutes and record all the ideas that come to your mind. Ideas may be about personal goals or business ventures. You may get thoughts and ideas you may not understand. Record everything, even things that may not make sense to you at the moment. This is where you are actually creating something out of nothing.

When you stop recording your ideas, read/listen to what you captured and think why you recorded what you did. Your first ideas are usually what you really desire. Take the time to think and reflect as to how each of these ideas is related to your desire to be and do – then for each idea, establish in your mind the exact goal you want to accomplish and be as precise as possible. As an

36

example, desiring to travel is not enough. You need to record where you want to travel, when, with whom, etc. You should chose ideas that will motivate and inspire you and are so big and worthy for you they will consume you and you will not want to spend time on things that do not matter, or listen to people who don't have the time to live or don't want to support you.

Always remember, every present moment is an opportunity for creation. Don't focus on the future and think "tomorrow, I will". The present moment is the perfect time to create and take action. Live in the present, be positive and happy, and stop prejudging people and yourself based on the past and what has happened. Start with a clean slate, and stay focused in the present moment.

Once you get the idea(s) into your conscious mind you want to focus on:

1. Use your imagination and you see yourself doing what you want.

    Imagination is where everything starts. You start imagining. You see it. You believe it. Then you do it.

2. Turn your idea into a goal. To turn an idea into a goal, ask: 1) Am I able to do it? 2) Am I willing to pay the price?

Am I able to do it?

You are someone who has unlimited possibilities, you are amazing, and you have a perfect mind. You are capable of doing anything you set into your mind and your answer to this question should always be without a doubt, a big YES! You may not know HOW you are going to do it, but you need to have confidence you will figure things out; and, you WILL. Believe and you will receive!

Am I willing to pay the price?

If you are not willing to pay the price, then it is definite you also do not deserve the positive results. The price you may have to pay depends on your goal. If the goal is to lose weight, then the price for losing weight is to exercise more. If the goal is to become wealthy, then the price may be to work more, and spend less time with your family. You never get something for nothing, and this is something you always need to have in mind. Determine exactly what you intend to give in return for the goal you desire, as there is no such a thing as a 'free lunch'. What you are willing to pay may be time, money, etc.

Once you answer these two questions, and you have determined exactly what you intend to give in return for the goal you desire, you have turned your idea into a goal and you can impress it upon your subconscious (emotional) mind. The way to do that is by using repetition and affirmations such as "I will accomplish that goal by the X date".

1. You develop a plan.

   You create a definite plan for achieving what you desire; then begin at once, whether you are ready or not, to put this plan into action. This is just so important. Many people wait for the right time to start something, but the right time never happens. You need to take action right away!

While you develop your plan, you need to establish a definite date as to when you intend to achieve your goal. Without setting a deadline, you risk procrastinating or letting other things to get in the way. By not setting a deadline, what you want, may actually never happen.

To put the plan in the subconscious mind, and turn your desire into a goal, create and record a clear and concise statement which will include the exact goal, what you are willing to give in return, and the deadline you have set up to accomplish the goal. In addition, describe clearly the plan through which you intend to achieve your goal.

Read your recorded statement aloud, twice daily, once before you go to sleep, and once when you wake up in the morning. Imagine, feel, and believe you have already accomplished your goal. [4]

What you may also want to do is to use a goal card. Write down your goal and carry the card with you wherever you go. As you read the goal, you get emotionally involved and it is only a matter in time for the goal to materialize. Use the present tense, as your goal has been already accomplished.

2. You apply your plan

You apply your plan again and again; you do not stop until you accomplish your goal. Application and taking action makes the difference, more than anything else. As you apply your plan, you have to keep on reminding yourself where you are going and believe you are going to get there. It might be scary sometimes but take one step at a time if you have too. [5] As Confucius said, "It does not matter how slowly you go as long as you do not stop." [6]

STEP 2 of two

Once you decide what you really want and desire, the second step is to look at current results and make a conscious decision you are not going to allow them to influence you. Your current results may lead you to have the following thoughts: "I cannot have, I cannot be, I cannot do this", or "It is not possible". The GOAL is what should inspire you to move forward, and not the present results! Everything should start by having a GOAL. CURRENT RESULTS do not matter! [7]

To realize the importance of this, you need to understand how people think, and how we are programmed by old habits and beliefs. This is what most people do:

1. We see the present results

2. The present results cause thoughts

3. Our thoughts cause feelings

4. The feelings cause actions

5. The actions cause more of the same results

If your present results are not good, then your thoughts will be negative; this causes negative feelings and then negative actions because we do not have confidence to believe in ourselves. We start all over again, looking at the present results. This eventually becomes a vicious circle.

Allowing present results, especially negative ones, to influence your thinking, puts you on a losing path. An ignorant person permits the appearance of things to control their thoughts and this is the last thing you ever want. [8]

You need to focus on the goal that motivates you and inspires you – not the present results.

How do we produce positive results?

Most people are trying to improve current results. When this doesn't happen, they get disappointed and start all over again, producing the same results.

If you want to produce positive results, this is what you need to do:

1. The starting point should be your ideas or goals. Start with your idea and what you really want.

2. Let the idea/goal dictate how you feel. The goal causes feelings.

3. How you feel will control how you act. The feelings cause actions.

4. How you act will produce the results you are getting.

That is how we produce results!

Then you look at the improved results; you adapt to the change, the circumstances and your environment, and you start with a new idea. Your new starting point becomes the new bigger and better exciting goal.

In a nutshell, when you apply the following three stages, you have the potential to create exactly the life you want:

1. Start by using your imagination and build images in your mind.

2. The images become ideas instilled in your subconscious mind by repetition.

3. Turn your ideas into a form by taking action.

"The starting point of all achievement is desire. Keep this constantly in mind. Weak desire brings weak results, Just as a small amount of fire makes a small amount of heat. If you find yourself lacking in persistence, this weakness may be remedied by building a stronger fire under your desires." [9]

– Napoleon Hill, Personal Success Author

"Take up one idea. Make that one idea your life – think of it, dream of it, live on that idea. Let the brain, muscles, nerves, every part of your body, be full of that idea, and just leave every other idea alone. This is the way to success." [10]

– Swami Vivekananda, Indian Hindu Monk

"First comes thought; then organization of that thought, into ideas and plans; then transformation of those plans into reality. The beginning, as you will observe, is in your imagination." [11]

– Napoleon Hill, Personal Success Author

"THE imagination is literally the workshop wherein are fashioned all plans created by man. The impulse, the DESIRE, is given shape, form, and ACTION through the aid of the imaginative faculty of the mind." [12]

"Ideas are intangible forces, but they have more power than the physical brains that give birth to them. They have the power to live on, after the brain that creates them has returned to dust." [13]

– Napoleon Hill, Personal Success Author

CHAPTER 5

MAKE THE DECISION

"Most of us are going through life without interrogating whether our decision-making processes are fit for purpose. And that's something we need to change – especially when the stakes are high and the decisions are of real import." [1]

– Noreena Hertz, English Academic, Economist, and Best-Selling Author

"We can use decision-making to choose the habits we want to form, use willpower to get the habit started, then – and this is the best part – we can allow the extraordinary power of habit to take over. At that point, we're free from the need to decide and the need to use willpower." [2]

– Gretchen Rubin, American Author, Blogger, and Speaker

The decision-making process is very easy for some people while for others it is extremely difficult. Some people even avoid making decisions at all costs, and they prefer to let others lead and make decisions on their behalf. The reality though is, whether it is for personal or professional reasons, we make decisions or we do not. On a daily basis, we may have to make big or small decisions that affect our lives. We need to make decisions as to what to eat, how to dress, where to live, who we allow to be our friends, and so on. And, even if we decide not to make a decision, that also is a decision!

Making decisions is inevitable and a necessary process in our everyday life. All decisions though need to align with our goals – if we want to move forward and accomplish what we desire.

When it comes to goals, there are two types of decisions you will need to take: a) the first decision is that you are going to change, b) the second type of decision you need to make is based on the ideas collected by the creative process.

Decision that you are going to change & common enemies

It always boils down to decisions and the first and most important conscious decision you have to make, is that **you are going to change**. That is what I did.

Until my mid-twenties I used to live in Greece. Even though I should have been happy living in such a wonderful place, there were so many things going wrong and I wasn't happy with my life. I didn't feel I was going anywhere with my job, financially I wasn't doing well, I was single, living in a closed-minded environment, and as a gay man I found it improbable I would ever find a life partner. I really felt alone and now I see I was deeply depressed for a long time.

One day, after feeling sorry for myself and not taking any type of action, I made the conscious decision I needed to change things. I didn't know yet what I needed to do, but I knew I was not happy with the way things were going. The decision to make a change came from within. I felt it with every part of my being.

After a lot of thought, I realized I needed to change everything in my life I didn't like. I was ready for a change and all the consequences that come with it, good and bad as they may have seemed at that time – that included cutting friendships I wasn't happy with, leaving my job, moving to another country, etc. I made a clear decision I had to take drastic measures and make a change, I stuck to it, and I knew there was no way I was going back to what it was before. I made such drastic changes; I actually feel I rewired my brain to discover new paths and opportunities not obvious to me before. Looking back, I know I changed my life not because I changed country, a job, and stopped any contact with people who didn't motivate me, but because I made a conscious decision inside of me I would change things. **If you do not make the decision to change inside you and feel it, then nothing happens.** Making such a definite decision was hard, it took a lot of courage, and internal fighting, but I knew I was doing the right thing.

You need to make a quick and definite decision you are going to change and stick with it the way I did. During the decision-making process remember people do not resist change, but being changed. People, who fail to accomplish their goals, have the habit of reaching decisions, if at all, very slowly, and also have the habit of changing these decisions quickly and often.

Your biggest enemy in making a decision is procrastination. As you procrastinate, you let days, months and years passing while wondering "what if?" You need to make the decision to change, and take action right away.

All you need to do to change things is to make a decision. To change your life, you need to make the decision you will change your life! [3]

Decisions on the ideas collected based on the creative process

During the creative process you will come up with many ideas that inspire you and you would like to explore further. Once you have written down all your ideas, prioritize and decide which idea you would like to take on first.

Even though it is true many of us can multitask and accomplish many goals at the same time (example: have a career while raising kids, while keeping a healthy body, etc.), to be as effective as possible – at least at the beginning – we need to focus on one goal at a time. This is very important, especially if our idea/goal is so big that it may consume all or most of our time. At the beginning, this is where we put the most effort, we learn as we go, and we pave the way so we can enjoy the fruits of our effort at a later stage. If our personal goal is, for example, to start and maintain an exercise/training program and we have never exercised before, it will take more time at the beginning for our body to adjust, but things will become easier later. If, in another scenario, you are building a business on your own, it will take you more time at the beginning to set up the business, but things will get easier at a later stage as the business grows, processes are established, and you hire employees and other people who contribute to your expansion. If you plan everything the right way, the hours you put into it may be reduced while your profits may be increased.

Making the decision is about deciding what it is you want to take on first, and committing that you are going to take action. What is important to you and what matters the most? What is it that touches you, moves you, and inspires you? Make the decision and do not let others influence you, or tell you that you cannot accomplish your goal. After all what is their qualification to judge and influence your decision, how bad do they want what you want, and how much are they willing to take a risk, and pay the price of going after what you want?

Decisions and opinions of others

The majority of people who fail to accomplish their goals are generally easily influenced by the "opinions" of others. They are just about to blossom, and then they permit the media, or in small communities the "gossiping neighbors" and acquaintances they don't even care about, to do the "thinking" and make the decisions for them. From one moment to the other, the excitement becomes disappointment, when you haven't even tried to go after what you want just because someone said "you will not be able to do it." Words from others have a mysterious way of getting deep in our minds, becoming saboteurs; it is our responsibility to ignore them when we know for a fact they do not benefit us.

"Your time is limited, so don't waste it living someone else's life. Don't be trapped by dogma – which is living with the results of other people's thinking. Don't let the noise of others' opinions drown out your own inner voice. And most important, have the courage to follow your heart and intuition." [4]

– Steve Jobs, Cofounder, Chairman, and CEO of Apple Inc.

If you ask a question of 100 people, everyone will have an opinion and will give you an answer. "Opinions" are the cheapest commodities on earth; everyone has an opinion about anything, ready to enforce that opinion on anyone who is ready to accept it. Many times because we want to feel socially accepted, we agree with opinions that do not necessary represent us. If you are influenced by "opinions" of others when you reach decisions, then it's almost a sure thing you will not succeed in any undertaking, and you will have no desire of your own.

Trust yourself, make your own decisions, and follow through by taking the appropriate actions. Take no one into confidence, except the people closest to you who you know for a fact are looking after your best interests, and are in complete sympathy and harmony with your purpose.

Commit to your decisions

Once you make the decision, then you need to commit to that decision. By committing, you materialize a thought to your reality and this is where everything starts. You also need to have something at stake that you may lose. If you want to travel, give a deposit now. If you want to go to the gym, register now. Make the decision and instead of keeping your intentions to yourself, make them known to many. Other people can help reinforce your behavior and this will keep you motivated. After all, it's harder to abandon a dream when you know that people are tracking your progress. Find a friend who can hold you accountable, and when you do not do something you promised you will do, ask them to call you on it. Dream big, even if that something seems totally impossible. Remember often it takes the same effort to accomplish something big as it will take to accomplish a small goal.

When you make the decision to change your life, ask yourself "What do I REALLY want?" and NOT "What do I think I can do or afford". Most people, when they set up goals, play it safe and set up goals based on what they know how to do. Stop going after things you know how to do and focus on the things you really want to have, do, experience and accomplish. As you make the decision that you will go after what you really want – and not after the things you know how to do, you should be willing to take risks to move forward. By doing that, you are opening the door to live a life full of excitement and possibilities.

CHAPTER 6

SET CLEAR GOALS

"People with clear, written goals, accomplish far more in a shorter period of time than people without them could ever imagine." [1]

– Brian Tracy, Author

Motivation is short-lived and doesn't always lead to consistent action. If you want to move forward, you need to make sure your goals are clear and you develop a plan as to how you will achieve your goals and by when. [2]

Visualize the goals you want to accomplish and record them. Be as precise as possible. Setting up a vague goal such as, "I want to buy a car" is not good enough. You need to decide what type of car you want (example: sports or sedan), if the car will be new or used, what brand the car will be and what color. Is the new car going to have accessories and how much money are you willing to spend? What is the deadline you are giving yourself to buy the car? For each goal, record all the details you think are important. By setting up clear goals, you help visualize your dreams and you bring them closer to your reality.

When you set up your goals, remember the word "SMART".

This is a well-known and well-used method designed to create actionable goals and is a system of goal identification, setting, and achievement. Used by life coaches, motivators, HR departments, and educators, each letter of the SMART method stands for an adjective that describes an effective way to set goals. [3] Your goals should be:

Specific

Measurable

Attainable

Relevant

Timely

Specific: When you set up a goal, you have to make sure your goal answers the following questions. WHO is going to do WHAT, WHEN, and to WHAT EXTENT? For example, instead of saying "I want to travel", the goal should be "In July 2017, I will travel with my husband to London, UK, we will stay for two weeks and we will spend our time visiting museums."

Measurable: When you set up your goal, you need to make sure you will be able to measure it and track its progress. The goal to lose 5 pounds within a month is measurable, versus the general goal to lose weight. [4]

Attainable: Your goal should be realistic. Even though I believe we can accomplish anything we put in our mind, we need to assess our current situation and give it the appropriate time until we accomplish it. If the goal is to finish a marathon that starts in a week from now, and you have never run before nor have an athletic background, the goal is probably not realistic. If the goal though is to finish a marathon a year from now and you are committed to start training every day, then the goal is attainable.

Relevant: You need to see the big picture; ask yourself if the goal is relevant to your life, who you want to be, and what you want to accomplish. Questions you may want to ask yourself are: do I really want to do this? Will I be able to pay the price and devote the time needed? Is now the right time for this? Does it seem worthwhile? Does it match my actual needs and the "big picture"?

Timely: Even though many of us do not like deadlines, setting a "due date" helps you keep track of the goal and manage "roadblocks" that get in the way. Instead of thinking "I'm going to increase my income", setting the goal "I will increase my income by 10% within 1 year" makes the goal time sensitive and more realistic.

When your action plan includes well-written goals, it is easier to develop crucial time-phased action steps. Depending on the goal, important information as to what needs to be done next will start to reveal itself. If your goal is "In July 2017, I will travel with my husband to London, UK, we will stay for two weeks and we will spend our time visiting museums", then some of the next steps may include "start saving money for your trip", "find the hotel you want to stay at", "book in advance your airfare tickets to save money", "ask your boss to give you your vacation on the dates you will be away", etc. If your goal is "to travel", then you will not know what to do next and where to start.

Setting **SMART** goals, taking action and staying disciplined every day will be much easier for you, while you will feel a great sense of achievement.

Here are a few additional things to consider when you are setting up and executing goals:

1. **Prioritize your goals:** Your time-sensitive and most important goals, or goals you badly want to happen, should be at the top of your list. For example, if you want to apply for a scholarship and the deadline ends in 3 days, then this goal becomes a top priority.

2. **Break the goal down into smaller pieces:** Very often, people give up as they feel overwhelmed by the enormity of a goal they must accomplish. Breaking the goal into small pieces, will make it easier to manage and be successful. This technique has been extremely helpful while I have been writing this book. The thought of writing a book initially overwhelmed me. It was like a huge elephant. Breaking the workload into very small projects, bite-size pieces, and focusing on each project/ chapter one at a time without thinking what is next made a huge difference. I devoured that elephant.

3. **Only work on one "major" goal at a time:** Your willpower is limited; when you work on many important goals at the same time, you lose energy, and eventually you lose motivation. Use your own judgment as to what YOU consider a major goal and how you can manage your energy levels and time to make things happen. We can manage many smaller goals at the same time – for

example, to lose weight while going to the gym while getting your university degree. If your goals though are a) to start a new business and make 2 million dollars in the first year while b) you are going full time to the university, then things may become very challenging. Focus on one big goal at a time. When that goal is accomplished, proceed to the next big goal.

4. **Don't be afraid to modify your goal or the steps towards that goal:** While you are working towards your goal, you may find out you have to adjust your goal to make it workable or to change the steps you have already planned towards that goal. You always have to evaluate and make adjustments as to what works and what doesn't. Do not be afraid to change and shake up things when they do not go exactly the way you want them. Change is inevitable and not adjusting is what makes us stay behind. If you have been planning to take a long trip and for any reason it cannot happen, then you need to make the commitment you will do the trip at a later date rather than just giving up. Also do not be afraid to change your approach towards accomplishing your goal. Think of poker players. Many times, to change their luck they go to a different table. All you have to do is to try something different that can take you closer towards accomplishing your goal.

5. **Dream big and set up goals that scare you and you think are impossible:** By going after attainable goals, doesn't mean you should not dream big or go after goals that for some may seem impossible to accomplish. You need to set up your own rules and believe the "impossible"

can happen. What is the one thing you want the most? Go after it. I'm often amazed with things around us we take for granted. We have wireless internet, huge planes fly through the sky, we video chat with our friends and families who live on the other side of the world. All those things, when you think about them, seemed a few years ago impossible to happen, yet now they are part of our daily life.

6. **Do not let others distract you from your goal:** Everyone has an opinion as to what we need to do and how to live our lives. Even though opinions should be respected, deep down you know more than anybody else what you want and why you want it. Avoid people who can distract you from your goal, and stay close to the ones who will support you, guide you, and mentor you.

7. **Focus on your goal and do not allow situations and circumstances to affect you:** The second we react to situations and circumstances of other people, they become in charge of us and we lose our focus on what really matters to us. This is the only life we have, it is short, and we make the mistake of putting other people and their drama in charge of us! Make the choice to focus on what you want rather on what is happening around you.

8. **Become obsessed with your goal:** Write your goal on a card and carry the card with you, all the time. Read the card many times throughout the day and set your mind on visualizing the final outcome of the goal. That may be, thinking of the money you want to make, the

promotion you want to have, the vacation you want to take, etc. Once you write your goal on paper you have to think how you are going to do it. Do not spend any time thinking you can't, think only how you can. You can do it if you decide to do it. Do not say "I do not know how". You will figure things out. Things will not happen, unless you decide they will happen. Having your goal become your purpose and obsession, means it is just a matter of time until you make it happen.

9. **Celebrate accomplishing your goal:** You know better than anyone else, how hard you have worked to accomplish your goal. When you finally accomplish what you have been trying to achieve, you should celebrate with every inch of your being the well-deserved results. By celebrating our victories, we motivate and set ourselves up for bigger and better goals. [5]

CHAPTER 7

THINK POSITIVE

*"Who told you it couldn't be done? And what great
achievement has he to his credit that entitles him to use the
word 'impossible' so freely?"* [1]

– Napoleon Hill, Personal Success Author

You made the decision you are going to make a change. You know which goals you are going to go after. As you are getting ready to take action, there are seven things you need to consider which may influence the level of your success. Collectively, these factors may influence your motivation and help you reach your goals, OR prevent you from accomplishing your goals. They are:

1. Positive Thinking

2. Awareness

3. Believing

4. Willpower

5. Happiness & Gratitude

6. The Power Of Love

7. Taking Care Of Body

In this chapter, we analyze the importance of positive thinking and what you can do to change negative thoughts to positive, and keep yourself motivated.

Thinking positive and focusing on what you want will bring you closer to what you desire. Imagining what you want, initiating, reaching out, and creating, as well as attracting others and taking action in line with those desires, are all the right and necessary steps in bringing your desires to reality.

Even though you may be laser-focused on your goal, it is almost a certain thing as you are executing your plan, things may not always go your way. Depending on your goal, you may not meet your deadlines, you may not get funding right away for your project, you may not manage to go to the gym every day as you are committed to do, and a million other things may happen. This is the time old habits, shaken willpower, and common enemies of procrastination, doubt, and fear may reveal themselves and try to influence you and sabotage you. As a result, you may lose your motivation and giving up is the first thing that will come to mind. Stop; take a deep breath or several.

What you always need to remember is YOU are the master of your own destiny, and you have the power to switch your mind and **think positive** despite the circumstances. Persistence and commitment to think positive under any circumstances, is what makes all the difference. Your challenge, and what you need to practice constantly, is to evaluate if a situation is actually negative and not just a product of your own negative thinking. If you evaluate a situation as negative, then the next step is to turn any negative thoughts related to that situation into positive thoughts and outcomes. In the meantime, you have to put yourself in a state of mind where you appreciate and welcome in your life all experiences; be open-minded enough to explore and figure out what you are getting even from those experiences you do not like. Remember, we are who we are through all the people whom we have met, and through the negative and positive experiences we have accumulated so far. Negative experiences are always a perfect opportunity to learn, grow, and master our ability to turn complaints into new possibilities.

As master of your destiny, you can – in just a moment – change any negative thinking into positive. The fundamental part of the process is to constantly monitor your thoughts. Every time you realize there is a negative thought that stops you from doing the things you want or discourages you, it is your obligation to change it. All it takes is a moment to make the switch. Be prepared to let go of negative thoughts; practice every day until it becomes second nature to you.

How do you stop unpleasant/negative thoughts?

Unpleasant thoughts are usually based on the fear that we are letting ourselves down, letting other people down, or simply not fitting into what is considered to be the social norms and expectations.

Recent research has indicated for humans it is more important to feel we are a valued and loved member of a relationship, a family, group, or community than being competitive with each other. Whether it is family, friends, co-workers, or a sports team, humans have an inherent desire to belong and be an important part of something greater than themselves. This implies a relationship that is greater than simple acquaintance or familiarity. The need to belong is the need to give and receive affection from others.

When our need to belong is challenged by negative thoughts, the first step to stopping those unpleasant thoughts is to talk to those whom you think you're disappointing or whom you will let down. While you are talking to them, share your thoughts and concerns, be genuine and authentic, and come from a place where you understand the point of view of the other person, and admit where you have been wrong while standing up for what you believe in. Even though it is not often obvious to us, because we are too close to see the big picture, ultimately, we're "all in this together". Everyone wants happy relationships, a happy life, and things to work out. When you are honest, authentic, speak from your heart, admit when you have been wrong, and are eager to take responsibility, others will ease your fears, and that fear disappears.

In some cases, some 'unpleasant thoughts' can be caused by others having small-minded beliefs, fears, or expectations about you. The real challenge is to identify the source of that negative thinking. Is the negative thinking caused by you, or by the negative beliefs of others? Try to be objective as much as possible and evaluate the situation. When the negative thinking is caused by others, their negative thoughts towards you reveals they're more in need of help and understanding than you are. Knowing this can greatly relieve 'unpleasant thoughts' when due to disapproval by others – as their disapproval often speaks more about them, than you.

If the unpleasant thoughts are about you, you need to remember the mind is what makes everything. There is nothing wrong with you and you are absolutely perfect. When you catch yourself unmotivated, or have thoughts that hold you back, you need to acknowledge those negative thoughts and focus on changing the state of your mind.

There are a number of things you can do to change negative thoughts into positive, and keep yourself motivated. The following are for generic negative thinking; they should not be equated with anxiety and depression. Anxiety and depression are real conditions needing caring treatment and medical help. These are some of the ideas you can use to improve your positive thinking: [2]

- **Try to think more about things that make you happy.** This is the miracle of positive thinking. When you focus on the things you like, enjoy doing, and make you happy, you are putting yourself on a different frequency and eventually you are thinking only positive things and rarely anything negative.

- **Be conscious and monitor your thinking.** Anything negative that comes into mind, replace instantly with something positive.

- **Record a list of all the things you really want.** Then every day focus on those things. Who do you want to be and what do you want to accomplish? By doing this, you're redirecting your energy into everything you want to bring into your life, rather than letting your negative thoughts take over.

- **Try meditation.** During meditation the body and mind calms and helps you reject any negative thoughts.

- **Try mindful meditation.** Mindfulness is a mental state achieved by focusing one's awareness on the present moment, while calmly acknowledging and accepting one's feelings, thoughts, and bodily sensations. When you are focused on the present moment, anything negative that doesn't matter will eventually go away.

- **Imagine you already have what you want.** Visualize how it will feel having what you want, and allow emotions and enthusiasm to take over. Use props to enhance your imagination and play the way kids do. Have fun with it.

- **Put visual cues on anything you see often.** (e.g., the mirror in your washroom) This will remind you of your goal and what you want to accomplish. Visual cues may include a picture of the body you want, the car or house you want, or simply words and sentences that will encourage you, empower you, and motivate you.

- **Change your outlook in life; start seeing challenges as opportunities.** Always remember anything negative that may happen to you is an opportunity to learn and grow.

- **Live an optimistic life.** Try new things, be aware and present, read motivational books or read about things that can spike your interest and inspire you. Explore your creative side, spend time with optimistic people, set meaningful goals, and don't forget to have fun! Laugh loud, laugh often.

- **Follow your inner voice, instincts, and intuition.** When we have negative thoughts, maybe there is something trying to tell us what we want may not be the best thing for us at that specific point of our life. Often we are not able to realize that until some time has passed and have the opportunity to see our situation from a different perspective.

- **Face your fears.** The secret to your freedom from fear is to realize you do not have to believe the voice in your head telling you "what if?" Instead, you can just observe that voice and say in your mind "thank you for sharing". Eliminate your fears by trying every day something that scares you and allow your decisions to come from the possibility of joy and growth, rather than fear.

- **Start your day with positive affirmations and happy thoughts.** When you do that, you set yourself up for a great day, and anything negative that may happen affects you in the least possible way.

- **Stop listening in your head to the voices of others who tell you not to do something.** No one else but you knows what is good for you, and what you can and you cannot do. Don't live with the limitations of others.

- **Visualize how it will feel if you do not get what you**

want. Imagine the pain, what you will lose; turn that energy into determination and persistence.

- **Change the language that limits you.** Replace your "but's" with the word "and", and "I can't" with the phrase "How can I?" As an example: "I want to buy a new car <u>but</u> I do not have the money" will be replaced with "I want to buy a new car <u>and</u> I have the money" or, "I can easily save the money".

- **Focus on the present rather than thinking about what has happened in the past, or worrying about the future and what may come.** Don't let bad past experiences impact today's thinking and outlook. Learn to acknowledge what happened without letting it interfere with the present. In addition, if you are constantly worrying about the future, you do not give yourself the chance to live and enjoy the present. As much as we may want, sometimes we cannot predict or control the future; many times we worry for no reason.

- **Be positive to attract anything positive.** When you are kind, helpful, and treat people with respect, most definitely you will receive the same treatment in return. Positivity attracts positivity, so make sure you treat people the way you want to be treated. Remember, if you do something positive, it will come back to you ten-fold – it works the same when you do something negative.

- **Stay physically fit and eat healthy.** When we feel strong and healthy, it is much easier to have a positive outlook in life.

- **Gratitude helps us maintain positive thinking.** Show gratitude and appreciate all the great things you already have in your life. [3]

- **Having a sense of control over your life is an important part of positive outlook thinking.** To maintain control, you need to stop comparing yourself with others, and how much control others may have in their life. When you compare yourself with others, you may get the impression they have more control in their life, than they actually do. This is a negative type of thinking and it may stress you for no reason.

- **Challenge all of your negative thoughts.** Monitor your thinking, and when automatic negative thoughts pop up, acknowledge them and start challenging them by asking questions like, "Is this situation as bad as I'm making it out to be?", "How does it benefit me to think negatively?", "Am I thinking negative based on actual facts, or based on my fears?" Then, replace the negative thoughts with positive thoughts. Confronting your negative thoughts may be challenging at the beginning but once this becomes a habit, you will automatically challenge them and replace them with positive thoughts.

- **Read books** about positive thinking, **listen to music** that inspires you, or **watch videos** that will motivate you to go after what you want.

- **Beautiful landscapes and pleasant comfortable weather calms our mind and helps us think positive.**

Make it a habit to visit beautiful places, and when the weather permits, go out to enjoy a pleasant day.

- **Avoid types of thinking that promote negativity.** [4] This includes:

  - ✓ **Black and white thinking:** This is when you see everything as very positive or very negative.

  - ✓ **Personalizing:** This is thinking where you automatically see everything that goes wrong as your fault.

  - ✓ **Filter thinking:** Here you choose to hear only the negative message in something communicated to you; instead listen for gold and what is positive.

  - ✓ **Catastrophizing:** This is when you can't think of anything without assuming it's all going to end in disaster.

- **Laugher and happy emotions are an important part of having a positive outlook.** Laugh often, have fun, enjoy life. Even when things are difficult, laugher can help us keep positive and get out of a negative situation.

- **Visualize what you would like to experience.** What and how you see yourself and your surroundings makes a difference to your thinking. Since we are thinking in pictures, change your mental pictures and start visualizing what you would like to experience.

- **Do things that spark your creativity.** Creativity is a

force for feeling positive as it inspires and leads you to continue discovering, making, and achieving in a never-ending loop. Creative people are able to see things most of us can't. They use their creativity and imagination to do things that seem impossible and find solutions to problems that seem difficult to solve. Creative people do not give up; they know they will find a way to accomplish what they want.

- **Let go of your negative thoughts using games and your imagination.** If you have a problem letting go of your negative thoughts, play games and use your imagination. Just take a handkerchief, hold it in the air and let it drop. The handkerchief represents all negative thoughts; by letting it drop, you are making a decision you are going to switch your mind to something positive.

- **Celebrate your victories.** When we celebrate our victories, we are changing our frequency, the way we feel; eventually we attract more positive things to come our way. Record a minimum of 5 accomplishments every day (yes, catching the bus on time on a raining day is an accomplishment as well) and celebrate each victory the best way you can.

CHAPTER 8

AWARENESS

A wareness is defined as, "the state or ability to perceive, feel, or be conscious of events, objects, or sensory patterns." [1]

There are two things you need to know to make a big difference in your life and accomplish your goals. You have to know where you are, and you have to know where you are going. Imagine for a moment you are a castaway on a remote island. You do not have any form of communication to reach the outside world, but you have a boat and you can use it to go back home. You are only 20 miles from the closest coastline that will take you back to the civilization, but you do not know that. If you go east, you will find civilization, but if you go west, you will take yourself towards the middle of the ocean where there is nothing but water. In this case you need to use any tools available – a map, a compass, and the stars – that can help you understand where you are before you take any further steps. Reaching out towards your goals is not much different. If you do not know where you are, it is not easy to see where you are going.

You have to take responsibility, see where you are in your life, and with honesty to answer these four questions:

1. Who am I?

2. What am I doing?

3. What works?

4. What doesn't?

Once you answer the four questions with honesty and integrity, things will start changing. You will change your thinking and you will go after your goals with deep clarity.

What we should be seeking is bigger and better goals and greater awareness – as this is the only way to improve results. Then everything else will happen.

An aware person thinks what they want to think, regardless of appearances, and stops him/herself from having negative thoughts and what comes with them – inability to experience the world and other people, and shutting down on being present. By allowing yourself to expand **your awareness and be present at the moment, be calm, notice people, listen attentively, feel the things happening to you with grace and care, you become aware of the obvious opportunities that surround us – you can make your life significantly more positive.** When we lack awareness, we miss the opportunity for change or the opportunity to achieve our goals. You have to be aware you are in the right place, at the right time, to go after what you want.

How do we increase our awareness?

There are two very important things to help you increase your awareness level

1. **Effective goals.** These are the bigger and better goals which motivate us and inspire us to move to increasingly higher levels of awareness.

2. **Knowledge.** Educating ourselves and being aware of the things around us increases the levels of our awareness. This demands we become lifelong students where we study every day and expand our minds.

It is very important to understand living in knowledge or ignorance can make all the difference between becoming successful or not.

Effects of living in ignorance [2]

When you live in ignorance, many things may happen that can affect your mental state and eventually your overall health. The road from ignorance to ill health can be catastrophic, yet preventable. This is how it works:

- Most of us, when we don't understand something, have doubts, and worry.

- Worry creates fear.

- Fear is expressed through the body and causes anxiety.

- When anxiety is not expressed, it turns into depression.

- Depression turns into disease and eventually to ill health.

You can fight ignorance by educating yourself, and developing an understanding about those things related to your goal. If your goal is to buy a new house, then you study and get a better understanding of the local real estate market. If your goal is to become wealthy by playing the stock market, then you educate yourself about stocks and you get a better understanding how the stock market works. You eliminate ignorance by educating yourself and becoming a life-long student.

Effects of living in knowledge [3]

You want to develop understanding as to how things work, and this can happen only by studying. This does not necessarily mean you need a university or college degree. Education in this instance is about finding information, learning and understanding everything in direct relationship with your goal.

- When there is understanding, you build faith which is the opposite of fear.

- Faith is expressed through your physical well-being.

- Physical well-being becomes clear thinking and high performance.

- While you are at this level of high-self, your mental state of mind and physical strength helps you build bigger and better goals; it helps you acquire the confidence you want to go after what you want.

When you are educated, you are at ease, and when you are at ease, your mind opens letting creative thoughts flow into your mind. As you become very creative, things happen. This process is called creation.

What else can we do to be mentally aware? [4]

These are some of the things which help you increase your awareness:

1. Do **mental exercises**. Playing chess, or using online tools and websites like Lumosity can be a great help. 5 minutes a day, of mental exercises may be enough.

2. Drink a lot of water; **avoid dehydration** especially at times you need to be aware.

3. **Exercise** every day, even if it is just for 10 minutes.

4. Incorporate some form of **quiet time** in your life – try to spend time with yourself without any type of disruption.

5. **Sleep** is very important. Make your environment comfortable and aim for constantly and consistently getting a good night's sleep.

6. Start **paying attention** to little things. Paying attention to little things first, will lead to your learning all the facts and increase awareness. Increase your curiosity about how things work, and often ask questions.

7. **Do first the things you do not want to do.** The sooner you eliminate from your schedule the things you do not want to do and you feel drain you, the sooner you can take them out of your mind and focus on the things that really matter. This eventually will work to your benefit.

8. **Plan all the time**. It's said the most valuable employees are those who can plan a large amount of information very quickly. You do not have to start by making big plans. Start little by little, and make successful plans, until this becomes a habit and a way of life. The closer

you get to that point, the easier it becomes to be more aware of all the facts of a situation.

9. **Breathing helps awareness.** Often our minds wander with things that happened in the past or things we want to do in the future. Breathing assists in cultivating awareness, and awareness keeps us in a present state so we may become aware of our surroundings. When we focus on our breath, the mind rests and awareness occurs. This is because, while the mind rests, you develop the ability to handle stress. [5] By eliminating stress you can respond effectively to various situations that cross your path. An additional benefit of breathing exercises is you bring in much needed oxygen to the body and in exhaling you remove toxins. This is a key feature of Mindfulness Practice.

That basic breathing practice can be used throughout the day, especially during times of stress. Called the **Four Square Breathing Technique,** it's done as follows:

- Inhale the breath for a count of four.

- Retain the breath for a count of four.

- Exhale the breath for a count of four.

- Pause for a count of four; repeat.

Repeat the practice a few times; breathe deep from the lower belly (feel your belly rise), instead of shallow panting from the upper chest. [6]

10. **Practice mindfulness mediation.** Mindfulness is a mental state where we are aware of whatever is happening in the present moment – accepting our feelings, thoughts and bodily sensations without judgment. Mindfulness is about knowing what you are experiencing while you are experiencing it, and allowing it to be whatever it is. You can achieve that state of mind by practicing mindfulness mediation – 20 minutes a day.

11. Embarrass your current situation with **kindness and acceptance.** Embarrass whatever is happening in that moment with kindness, without resistance; accept it without it needing it to be something different, or having a different outcome other than what it is.

CHAPTER 9

BELIEVE

*"Even when I was in the orphanage, when I was roaming
the street trying to find enough to eat, even then I thought
of myself as the greatest actor in the world. I had to feel the
exuberance that comes from utter confidence in yourself.
Without it, you go down to defeat."* [1]

– Charlie Chaplin, Actor, Director

Believing is the key to your success. Successful people believe in themselves no matter what, and they know that if they think they can, then anything is possible.

*"Man often becomes what he believes himself to be. If I keep on
saying to myself that I cannot do a certain thing, it is possible that I
may end by really becoming incapable of doing it. On the contrary, if
I have the belief that I can do it, I shall surely acquire the capacity to
do it even if I may not have it at the beginning."* [2]

– Mahatma Gandhi, Leader of Indian Independence Movement

If you want to be a successful best-selling author, then first you have to believe you are a successful writer. If you want to be a successful business man, then you have to believe you are already one. If you do not believe in yourself, then do not expect others to do so.

You need to live in a realm where anything is possible. Do not try to put it in a confined space because it creates boundaries. Start to believe in you and your goals, not because you really want it or it is your destiny to be successful, but because you know this is your purpose, and you are committed to do whatever needs to be done to make it happen. You know you are going to put in the work, and you will be patient and persistent. You know as long as you are breathing, you will continue towards who and where you want to be, and you know you will overcome any obstacles that come your way.

As Napoleon Hill said, "Whatever the mind can conceive, the mind can achieve" [3]. Be unreasonable, enthusiastic, talk with excitement about your goal, and believe no matter how big or small your goal is, anything is possible and you can make it happen. Believing comes from within; as long as you believe, you will receive as it has happened with many successful people before you. You just have to keep going until you get there.

Imitating the attributes of successful people is a good strategy to enhance your own beliefs and motivation. These are some of the attributes of highly successful people that help them achieve their goals:

- Successful people do not let anyone tell them they can't.

- They integrate their belief with their behavior. They say they believe in things and their behavior shows they really do.

- They have an optimistic outlook, reject from their mind anything telling them what they want will not happen, and believe everything will go as planned.

- They take a stand for what they believe, regardless of circumstances and possible lack of support. They believe, no matter what.

- They are willing to risk everything to do what they believe in.

- They see failure as opportunities to learn from mistakes to be successful next time. Edison famously said, "I have not failed 10,000 times. I have not failed once. I have succeeded in proving those 10,000 ways will not work. When I have eliminated the ways that will not work, I will find the way that will work." [4]

How To Develop A Belief In Ourselves

Believing in yourself is a state of mind which you may develop at will, and is the element which determines the action of your subconscious mind. How can we develop belief though when it doesn't already exist?

One way to do this is by conditioning your subconscious mind. Ask yourself. When you were a child, and you started walking, did you know how to do it? The answer is no. Through trial and error, and after many falls, you gained the confidence and the belief you could do it.

The same approach works with everything you want to accomplish. The first step is to gain the belief you can. Start applying what you want to accomplish on a smaller scale and get a taste of how it feels to have what you want. If, for example, you want to become an excellent financial advisor and manage the money of others, start by managing successfully your own money. Once you gain the belief you can do it, move forward and execute your action plan.

In his book "Think and Grow Rich", Napoleon Hill describes how to build belief using affirmations and autosuggestion. [5] This is my own interpretation based on the book and additional extended research.

Belief or faith, is a state of mind which develops voluntarily, through application and use. Repetition of **affirmation of orders** to your subconscious mind is the only known method of voluntary development of the emotion of faith.

You are "deceiving" your subconscious mind to believe, and you give it instructions through **autosuggestion**. To make the "deceit" more realistic, you conduct yourself, as if you have already in your possession the image you have created in your subconscious mind. You act as you already have the body you desire, the car you admire, or the person in your life you feel will make you happy. Perfection will come through practice, patience, and persistence.

What are affirmations though and what is autosuggestion?

Affirmations

Affirmations are statements aimed to affect the conscious and the subconscious mind.

The words composing the affirmation, automatically and involuntarily, bring up related mental positive images to mind; this motivates, inspires, and energizes you; it keeps your mind focused on the goal. Depending on what you want to accomplish, here are examples of affirmations: "I have a strong, healthy body", "I attract happiness in my life", "I'm a money magnet", "I'm a very successful person". Your statements need to be clear and concise. Repeating these affirmations affects your subconscious mind which in turn influences behaviors, habits, actions, and reactions. For example, changing your actions may bring you closer to people who may help you accomplish your goals.

As you embed those positive images into your subconscious mind, expect, at least at the beginning, resistance and struggle. We have been taught to believe there are certain things we cannot do. We were taught for various reasons and excuses things will not work out. The old beliefs, your negative thoughts and doubts, will tell you that you are not, and you cannot be, who you say you are. Persevere; do not let your negative thoughts and doubts conquer you.

Devote some special times during the day and repeat your affirmations. Repeat your affirmations aloud when you first wake up the morning and just before you go to sleep. The vibrations of your voice will send the message to the universe and will also get the message to your subconscious mind that in return helps you change your belief system and accomplish your goals. Repeat your affirmations hundreds of times during the day and for a minimum period of 21 days to establish a new belief and produce your results.

Autosuggestion

Autosuggestion is the medium for influencing, and embedding affirmations in your subconscious mind. By applying the principle of autosuggestion, you are giving orders to your subconscious mind with clear and concise statements. Example: "I'm a very successful person". By putting focus on these thoughts, you will eventually dominate your subconscious mind and manifest whatever you want into your life.

These are the steps to successfully autosuggest affirmations into your subconscious mind [6,7].

- **Repeat:** Repeat mentally or verbally what it is you wish to manifest. This is the most important rule in making successful suggestions.

- **Use images:** Verbal or mental suggestions are stronger when you attach an image. Use your imagination and plant that image to your subconscious mind.

- **Use emotion:** Words without emotion have no value. It is like repeating something you read somewhere and does not make any sense to you. Use exciting and emotional words that motivate and inspire you.

- **Use present tense:** Phrase your suggestions as though they were already an accomplished fact.

Autosuggestion can also be applied by using sleep as a tool. [8] This is what you need to do:

1. Record your autosuggestion with a strong and commanding, yet soft and gentle voice. If you don't like the sound of your voice, have a friend or family member record it.

2. Repeat your affirmation multiple times until you have a 30 minute recording.

3. Use the second person. Since you are commanding yourself, use the second person. For example, instead of saying "I am a great person, "say "You are a great person."

4. Once your recording is ready, find a comfortable room that doesn't have much noise and allow yourself to relax. Breathe deeply and regularly as you listen to your recordings.

5. Make sure you put the recording on repeat so it will play continuously while you're falling asleep.

6. Use the recording for 14 consecutive nights. Repetition will help you absorb the affirmation. After the 14-day period, move on to a new affirmation.

How to develop belief

In his book "Think and Grow Rich", Napoleon Hill [9], describes a self-confidence formula that helps develop belief. We can slightly alter the formula, if needed to serve our own purposes. This is my interpretation of his main points:

1. While you acknowledge you have the ability to achieve your goals, you demand from yourself to be persistent and take continuous action until that goal is accomplished.

2. You acknowledge your thoughts eventually transform into physical reality, and you commit you will spend 30 minutes a day, thinking of who you want to become and you build the mental image in your mind of that person.

3. In addition to your goal, to achieve in your life what's important to you, you will use autosuggestion to demand you develop your self-confidence.

4. While you have many smaller goals you want to accomplish, you have also clearly recorded a description of your main purpose in life, and you are committing yourself you will not stop trying until it has been achieved.

5. You will live a life based on integrity, truth, justice, and love. You will succeed by attracting to yourself the forces you wish to use, and the cooperation of other people. You will induce others to serve you, because you are willing to serve others and you will eliminate any negative attitude to others since you know it will not bring you success. You will cause others to believe in you, because you will believe in them, and in yourself.

You will sign your name to this formula, commit it to memory, and repeat it aloud once a day, with full FAITH it will gradually influence your THOUGHTS and ACTIONS so you will become a self-reliant, and successful person.

Believing in yourself, or not believing, can make the difference between accomplishing your goals and failing. It is that simple. You need to have laser-like focus, be persistent, and go ahead full speed. This is not the time to hold back. You are attracting everything that comes into your life, so do not afraid to step out of your comfort zone.

CHAPTER 10

WILLPOWER

"Willpower is the key to success. Successful people strive no matter what they feel by applying their will to overcome apathy, doubt, or fear." [1]

– Dan Millman, American Author and Lecturer

"The man who goes farthest is generally the one who is willing to do and dare. The sure-thing boat never gets far from shore." [2]

– Dale Carnegie, American Writer and Lecturer

"In the absence of willpower, the most complete collection of virtues and talents is wholly worthless." [3]

– Aleister Crowley, English Occultist

"Willpower is trying very hard not to do something you want to do very much." [4]

– John Ortberg, Evangelical Christian Author and Speaker

"The will is the keystone in the arch of human achievement. It is the culmination of our complex mental faculties. It is the power that rules minds, men and nations." [5]

– Thomas Parker Boyd, Founder of the Society of the Healing Christ

*"To assert your willpower is simply to make up your mind that
you want something, and then refuse to be put off."* [6]

– Phillip Cooper, Secrets of Creative Visualization

*"The will to win, the desire to succeed, the urge to reach your
full potential... these are the keys that will unlock the door to
personal excellence."* [7]

– Confucius, Chinese Teacher, Editor, Politician, and Philosopher

The importance of Willpower

Willpower is the ability to resist short-term temptations to
meet long-term goals, and is a special mix of determination,
persistence, and self-control.

We may have made the decision to change, and set up a clear
goal. By lack of willpower and inability to resist temptations,
we may prevent ourselves from achieving the outcome we are
looking for and reaching our full potential. Many people believe
they could improve their lives drastically, if only they had more
willpower. According to the American Psychological Association,
Americans name lack of willpower as the No. 1 reason they fail
to meet their goals.

How to Strengthen Your Willpower

Willpower is a muscle, which can be strengthened by **practicing
every day** and working on any goal or habit that exercises your
self-control.

Your willpower is strengthened not only by undertaking big goals, but also by doing anything that gets your brain out of its comfort zone – things like using your non-dominant hand instead of your dominant. Multiple studies have illustrated when you exercise self-control in one area of your life – such as brushing your teeth with your non-dominant hand – you can exert more willpower in another area, such as suppressing aggressive behavior. The two behaviors may be very different, but they share a common energy source. In the long term, you can strengthen your willpower by doing exercises that override habit.

How to conserve your willpower

While you can strengthen your willpower essentially only by practising every day, there are many other things you can do to conserve and boost your willpower. What follows are some suggestions, so you may get the extra push you need to achieve what you want:

1. **Watch what you eat and drink.** Willpower is a limited physiological resource powered by glucose. Our bodies draw on our store of glucose, which carries energy to the muscles and brain. When our glucose levels get low, our willpower weakens. You can boost your willpower reserves temporarily by ingesting glucose.

    To keep your willpower high, don't skip meals; eat regular meals, ideally low-glycemic foods full of healthy high proteins, vegetables and complex carbohydrates. The glucose will take an hour to get into your bloodstream, but you'll avoid a sugar crash and such foods are better for you in general.

If you need your glucose hit right away, especially if you need to make a big decision, eat something sugary, as this will get the glucose into your bloodstream and to your willpower supply quickly. You may take a bite of dark chocolate for a quick energy boost, or drink some juice.

2. **Don't make big decisions or start challenging tasks on an empty stomach.** Our brain is our decision-making muscle and its ability to provide us with the necessary willpower to make correct decisions is influenced by whether it is sufficiently fed. Exercising self-control depletes relatively large amounts of this glucose, and when glucose goes down, so does your willpower. If you are on an empty stomach, then you do not have sufficient glucose in your body; as a result your willpower is reduced and you are making poor decisions.

   This is why you should never go into anything important, such as a meeting with an important client, an interview, or a test on an empty stomach. However, while you should not be on an empty stomach, you also need to keep balance and not eat so much you will feel uncomfortable.

3. **Avoid excess amounts of alcohol.** Alcohol impairs our judgment, reduces our self-awareness, and impedes our willpower. Avoid consumption of excess amounts of alcohol, especially if you're in a situation where you have to exercise willpower. [8]

4. **Don't try to work or make important decisions when you're sick.** When you're sick, your immune system pulls glucose from your body, including your willpower supply, to fight off the infection. By having a low supply of glucose, the probability you will make poor decisions is higher. If you try to work, you do not help yourself and you make the recovery period longer.

5. **Remember your goals.** If your willpower feels drained, think of the task at hand as a necessary stepping stone to help you achieve your goals. If as an example you do not like filing, see it as a necessary task to get organized and build a successful business.

6. **Limit your choices.** Making big decisions, you can waste a lot of willpower; having too many choices has the exact same effect. Pursuing perfection, you end up with nothing, instead of something that would have made you happy. To understand this, think of the times you went shopping and there were too many choices or when you went to a buffet restaurant where you couldn't decide what to eat. The best way to conserve your willpower is to figure out the criteria for what you want and when you find something that makes you happy stick with it. This applies to everything in life including your relationships, business decisions, products and services you buy, etc.

7. **Get a good night's sleep.** After a long day, your willpower is low and your capacity for impulse-control is diminished. Self-control requires brain power, and when we are tired, our bodies generally don't deliver enough glucose to our brains. Rest reduces the body's need for

glucose, and it allows the body to make better use of what we have. It is absolutely amazing what a good night's sleep will do. Problems that felt all-consuming the night before will seem completely insignificant when you get out of bed. Adequate rest is generally 7-8 hours a night for an adult, and 10-12 hours a night for a child.

8. **Practice Mindfulness Mediation (as little as 8 weeks, even 5 minutes a day).** Kelly McGonigal, Ph.D., who teaches a class on The Science of Willpower at Stanford University, ranks meditation as the #1 way to increase willpower.

She says, "Practicing mindfulness meditation for a few minutes each day can actually boost willpower by building up gray matter in areas of the brain that regulate emotions and govern decision-making." [9]

Neuroscientists tell us meditation leads to a wide range of self-control skills, including greater attention, better focus, and more impulse control. Research also reveals meditators find it easier to lose weight or end an addiction.

When we become "mindful," [10] and we build self-awareness through mediation, we are also engaging that part of our brain we need for willpower, rather than just letting our impulses take over. Every time our mind wanders and we have to get it back on track, we have to tap into our reservoir of willpower. Take five minutes a day, focus on your breath. and detach yourself from anything that is going on around you. This simple act will help you be more aware and build your willpower. [11]

9. **Hack your mind with the 5-minute rule.** If you're struggling to get started on a project or activity you have to do (example: start your daily workout), make the following commitment with yourself:

I will do only 5-minutes and nothing more.

It is proven many times once you start, you are in action and you end up continuing past the 5-minute mark you had decided on.

10. **Don't keep yourself in a constant state of willpower exhaustion.** As we consider willpower a muscle you need to exercise, not letting that muscle rest will eventually burn it out and you will create the opposite results. Never giving yourself a break is a good way to deplete your resolve.

11. **Use your imagination.** Imagination is a powerful technique for improving willpower; your body responds to situations you are imagining exactly the same way as the ones you are experiencing. Practice and imagine situations where you will need to use increased willpower.

In addition, visualize yourself enjoying the fruits of your newfound self-control. Make a habit of asking yourself whether it's worth trading something you really value for a momentary pleasure.

12. **Think about something else.** You can use your imagination to keep unwanted thoughts away. This technique is very effective and I use it often when I exercise. When I reach my limits, and my mind tells me to stop, I focus and I think of something else to complete the task. Train yourself to think about something else. Every time unwanted thought threatens to intrude on your consciousness, think about something pleasant instead. [12]

13. **Do the opposite of what you normally do and exercise your willpower.** Exercise your prefrontal cortex by pushing past the resistance of your emotional response. Anytime you modify your routine, you're developing self-control. Do small things you do not normally do to strengthen your willpower. This will help you accomplish at a later stage something more substantive. These are some of the things you may want to try:

    • Try crosswords even though you may find them difficult;

    • Work on a tough-to-solve puzzle;

    • Watch a funny movie but resist the urge to laugh;

    • Watch a sad movie but resist the urge to cry.

    Reading informative books (and comprehending them) is another good way to exercise the cognitive efficiency of your prefrontal cortex.

Basically, do things (that are good for you) that provoke emotional resistance and break through that with persistence.

14. **Practice coping with stress.** Stress depletes willpower, so you need to develop good habits that will support you when a mild or major stressor comes along. These are examples of some good habits to help you during stressful times:

- Stop to take a few deep breaths (4 to 6 breaths per minute − 10 to 15 seconds per breath) when feeling overwhelmed or tempted, this is a great start in managing your stress levels and improving willpower.

- Listen to calming music.

- Practice mindfulness mediation as it helps you cope with stress and strengthen willpower.

- Visualize or view calming scenes.

- Watch comedies.

- Send surprise gifts and do anything that puts you in a good mood.

- Do moderate exercise or hot yoga.

15. **Only work on one goal at a time.** This is because your willpower is a finite resource; when you spend your

willpower on one thing, you have less available for other things. Try not to spread yourself too thin.

16. **Break down the goal into smaller pieces.** Often, people give up because they feel overwhelmed by the enormity of the goal they must accomplish. Breaking the goal into small pieces will make it easier to manage it and be successful. This technique has been extremely helpful in writing this book. The thought of writing a book initially overwhelmed me. Breaking the workload into very small projects, and working on each chapter, one at a time, without thinking and worrying what is next, has made a huge difference.

Breaking the goal into smaller pieces, taking action, and staying disciplined every day is much easier and you feel a great sense of achievement.

When you create your goals, make sure they are **SMART**:

Specific

Measurable

Attainable

Relevant

Timely

Here is an example of a **SMART** goal: I will complete

the 11th chapter of the book, by May 3rd. For more information about **SMART** goals I recommend you revisit Chapter 6 of this book.

17. **Stay away from temptation and create a plan to avoid challenging your willpower.** This approach is really simple. You need to avoid places, situations, things, and people that challenge your willpower.

   Staying away from temptation: You can do this by developing a system that will help you bulletproof yourself against potential distractions and sabotage.

   First, identify your common distractions. In my case, especially while I have been writing this book, my common distractions have been checking my work email, my Facebook profile, and reading the news, as I always want to know what is happening. Identifying your distractions is very important since those are the things that may trigger your willpower and you want to avoid. If you know, as an example, you have a problem with alcohol, keep it out of the house.

   Then build a structure to soften and even eliminate your distractions. Depending on the goal, there are different methods and strategies you can use. In my case, I eliminated internet access by turning off wireless access, and I used it only when I HAD to do research. In addition, I left my phone, on purpose, in another room. I made sure everyone in my house knew I was working and I made it clear they shouldn't interrupt me. The structure you want to develop should be different depending on your goal. If your goal is to lose weight, then the distractions you need to avoid should be different. Example: you need to avoid foods that are not healthy. If the goal is to start working on your tax return, you should not start on a day you know you will have a heavy schedule at work.

Create a plan, to avoid challenging your willpower: Your willpower is in limited supply. So, when you are mentally exhausted, there is a greater chance of succumbing to instant gratification. **It's best to plan and prepare for your times of low self-control.** You need to have a ready-made plan of what you need to do, in case you find the path of temptation.

The best way to deal with these types of situations is to follow an "If-Then" strategy. I will analyze this strategy in Chapter 16, but briefly the formula you should follow is this:

If [X Temptation], then I will do [Y].

Example 1: **If** [the phone rings], **then I will** [let it go to voice mail]

Example 2: **If** [everyone orders a pizza], **then I will** [resist and order a salad]

It's also a good idea to space out and prioritize multiple tasks; trying to do too many things at once will drain your willpower quickly and tempt you to procrastinate.

Creating a plan in advance, as to what to do when your willpower is challenged, can really make a big difference to successfully accomplishing your goal or not.

18. **Monitor your thinking.** Monitor your thinking and don't allow thoughts that can control your mind. Even though it is not always easy to do, sometimes you know one thought can lead to another and consume your time. If you are trying to finish a project and you see how wonderful the weather is outside, if you let it, the mind can easily start wandering. You need to focus and concentrate only on the task you need to finish.

19. **Exercise.** Exercise is a wonder drug for self-control and improving willpower. Not only does it increase our fitness and mental performance, improve our mood and sleep quality, reduce our body fat percentage and anxiety levels, and likelihood of becoming sick, but it calms us down, relieves stress, and acts as a powerful anti-depressant. [13]

   Find a type of exercise you love (example: running, swimming, yoga, or martial arts), and make it a regular part of your life. Even 5 minutes a day will make a difference but I recommend at least 30 minutes, 3 times a week. Exercising outdoors where you get fresh air and sunlight has additional obvious benefits.

20. **Eliminate unnecessary decisions.** Taking a lot of time to make small, unnecessary decisions dips into our willpower reserves. Eliminate or minimize small

and unnecessary decisions (as an example, what to eat and wear) and save your brainpower only for the most important decisions you have to take within the day. Taking 15 minutes to decide what you are going to wear at work just doesn't make sense.

21. **Do the most uncomfortable/challenging task at the beginning of the day.** Our willpower is at its highest in the morning, and progressively decreases throughout the day, as we constantly exercise our self-control and make decisions. [14] Knowing this, we want to manage our day so as to do our most difficult tasks at the beginning of our day, when we know we are in our highest capacity. Work on projects and tasks, and have the conversations you find the most challenging, at the beginning of the day. When you are having a test, solve the most difficult problems first. If in your personal life you have problems with your spouse or professionally you are facing issues with your boss, you need to make those important conversations at the beginning of the day, especially after you both had a good breakfast. If you delay those discussions for later, your willpower is low, your capacity for impulse-control is diminished, and you're likely to say things you'll regret.

As your goal should always be to reach high productivity – optimal or peak performance – you may want to apply a very well-known principle at the beginning of the day. Pareto's Principle says that 20% input gives 80% output. The 80/20 rule, should serve as a daily reminder to focus 80 percent of your time and energy on the 20 percent of your work that is really important. Don't just "work smart", work smart on the right things. For that reason, we should focus on doing the 20% of the most difficult tasks at the very beginning of the day.

22. **Choose a reward in advance.** Choosing a reward when you reach the end of your effort, helps you focus on the end goal rather than the activity and the effort you exert trying to accomplish the goal. Be generous with yourself and chose a reward that will motivate you and is something you really want.

23. **Unleash Your Inner Conquistador and Burn the Ships.** If you have a big project to complete, and you're struggling to discipline yourself, burn your ships.

What does that mean though?

Engineer a situation that will prevent you from retreating and will force you to get into action mode. [15] When I decided to write this book, I knew it would be challenging. I announced to everyone I knew I will write a book, and I had to take action right away to safeguard my integrity. Since I'm a man of my word I had to do what I said I will do.

24. **Go for the 100% commitment.** If we are not 100% committed to something, we are fighting internally, and our willpower challenges us. Questions arise such as: "Should I do this or I should not bother?", "Will I be able to make it happen?" etc. By being 100% committed, there is nothing to question and we focus only on the fact we have to take action.

25. **Set up an accountability system.** We often give ourselves excuses to not do something. "I have other priorities, I'm tired, and I don't feel like it, I do not have enough time, it's too much work, it's too hard, and I can't do it on my own."

We give ourselves these excuses because we are very comfortable with the situation we are in at the moment and we do not want to get out of our comfort zone. By allowing these excuses to dictate what we do, we do not allow ourselves to go after bigger and better goals and reach our personal greatness.

To avoid having excuses control what you do, you simply set up an accountability system that will hold you to a higher standard and prevent you from coming up with excuses. It's not only helpful to monitor your own progress, but to have someone else looking over your shoulder as well.

Here are some ideas to try while you build your own accountability system:

- get an accountability partner

- set an appointment to work out with a friend

- work side-by-side with a co-worker (or friend)

- hire a life coach

- join (or create) a mastermind group

- post your progress publicly on a blog or on Facebook

- use websites that help you set up goals and achieve them, like www.stickk.com

Whatever specific system you use, the most important thing is that it takes away your ability to procrastinate and make excuses, and that it makes you stick to your plan and highest values.

26. **Anticipate Roadblocks.** When you start pursuing a goal, consider what might interfere with your plans. Always assume roadblocks will come up and your motivation may weaken when they do. When we anticipate though the roadblocks in advance, when they actually arise, we have stronger willpower to deal with them. We see the roadblocks as a part of the original plan and the effect they may have on us is minimized.

27. **Search for the reason behind lack of willpower, and then let it go.** Beating ourselves up for not being able to maintain our willpower for a specific goal does not lead us anywhere or help us at all. First, we need to be kind to ourselves and acknowledge all the hard work we are doing. Then we need to figure out what that one thing is that's holding us back. Are we afraid of failing? Do we let insecurities prevent us from even trying? If what we are trying to do seems too much – we need to know it's normal to feel this way, and go through it anyways.

Fear of failure, workload stress, and peer pressure are among the most common root causes that hinder performance. If you feel as if you can't accomplish the goal, figure out the reason and overcome it. Unless and until you boost willpower in yourself, things won't change. [16]

28. **Delay gratification instead of eliminating it completely.** When you cut something out of your life completely, then the desire for it increases. By delaying gratification, you diminish the strength of the desire, and this allows you to be satisfied with less when you do indulge. This is one of the reasons the Pomodoro Technique (working for 45 minutes straight and then taking a 15 minute break) is so successful. [17] When you know you have a scheduled break/indulgence coming up, it becomes much easier to stick with a program without feeling overwhelmed by what you can't do or have to do at that moment.

29. **Have a higher purpose.** Having a higher purpose, avoiding instant gratification, and finding a reason for your goals that's deeper and less short-lived than the superficial, conserves your willpower and the decision-making process becomes a lot clearer. What will inspire you more? Do you want to become rich to have nice things, or do you prefer to help and do things for your family and the people you love? Do you want to build a fit body to look good for others, or do you want to build a healthy and strong body so you can potentially live longer?

Always remind yourself why you are doing something, and what it will actually cost if you quit.

30. **Keep yourself and your surroundings tidy and clean.** There is a strong connection between external order and the strength of your willpower. [18] People who take care of themselves and keep their surroundings tidy and clean, usually have higher willpower than others. You can use this approach as an exercise to build your own willpower.

31. **Monitor your behavior.** It's hard to practice willpower if you aren't aware of your current behavior and routines.

Most people are hiding themselves, from themselves, and they have only a very small idea of their behaviors, routines, and the impact those behaviors have on their lives. They are unaware how much time they spend online, how much food they eat, or how much money they spend. If you don't know where you're at in a certain pursuit, there's no way you'll reach your goal; you won't know what you need to change, how far you've come, and how far you have to go. If you do not know where you are, it will be very difficult to determine where you want to go and what to accomplish. You need to start monitoring your behavior by keeping a diary, or by using online tools to help you record and monitor your current behavior and progress. A record will help you track when, where, and why your progress slowed down (if ever), and when you are doing well, it will remind you to reward yourself on a regular basis for a job well done.

32. **Make to-do lists.** Once you finish a task, your brain mainly forgets about it. Those tasks though that are not finished, stay in your mind and your brain doesn't let them go until you do something about them. Those tasks end up consuming a lot of your willpower, even if they are at the back of your mind.

To get those tasks out of your mind, all you have to do is to put them on paper. The classic to-do list can really work wonders for your willpower. Be sure to make your list of to-do's as specific as possible and record the actions you are going to take, step by step. [19]

33. **Make changes during periods of calm.** Don't attempt big goals and habit changes when you've got a lot on your plate. The priorities that are unrelated to your big goal, will suck away your willpower, and leave you without enough of it to reach your big goal.

34. **Things will get easier.** When we struggle to accomplish a difficult task, we often forget that by repetition, practice, and resistance training the task will get easier. But, beware; as we are ready to reach a breakthrough, we give up.

To fight the desire to give up, we need to remember willpower, like a muscle, can be strengthened letting us get the energy to resist anything holding us back.

35. **Achieve balance.** Because on any given day we have a limited amount of willpower, it's important we use it wisely. Use your calendar; rank your activities in terms

of the energy or self-control they require. If you have to see a difficult client, do it on a day you do not have a busy schedule to protect your willpower.

36. **Create Powerful Habits, Rituals and Routines.** When you make decisions, you can consume a lot of your willpower. By creating rituals and daily routines, you can remove needless decision-making from your day. [20]

Once you have a set schedule for the day, a regular routine, and something has been turned into a habit, you don't even have to think about your task. You do it without using any of your willpower.

37. **Take frequent breaks.** As it is impossible to have perfect self-control all the time, when we are tired, we run the risk of making poor decisions. We need to refresh our mind and strengthen our willpower by taking frequent breaks, even if it is just for a few minutes. Getting something healthy to eat, taking a power nap, or watching TV for a few minutes may actually help you produce better work.

38. **Postponing things.** Postponing things to gain focus on what's important now, can be effective, especially if you're trying to break a bad habit (e.g.: smoking). [21]

39. **Connect with colleagues.** When you feel unmotivated or distracted, go talk to a co-worker or invite your colleagues to lunch. Working with people you care about, toward a common goal is a surprisingly effective way to restore your willpower. [22] Our willpower also increases when we feel recognized and appreciated for

our work. Seeking acknowledgment for a job well done can increase your willpower.

40. **Identify what you want willpower to achieve and keep it within reason.** Sometimes a lack of willpower can come from goals that are larger-than-life for the moment. Start with realistic bite-size short term goals to get you closer to what you want.

41. **Think positive.** Shame and embarrassment can undermine your willpower, so you need to consider your challenges in a positive light. If you're trying to lose weight, for instance, think of all the tasty and healthy things you can eat, rather than the long list of things you need to avoid. [23]

42. **Enjoy life.** Positive emotional experiences replenish your self-control reserve. So throughout the day – take a few moments to enjoy your life and do the things you absolutely love. [24]

43. **Self-Affirmations.** Similar to positive emotional experiences, self-affirmations have been shown to help replenish depleted willpower.

    According to a study published in the Journal of Personality and Social Psychology, self-affirmations can even help you to have more self-control when you're running out. [25]

44. **Rest.** When we reach that point where our reserve of willpower runs dry, we should not force it into override.

Set up all the necessary visual signals that send the message there is no decision to be made. Relocate to the bedroom, play calm music if this is what you like, turn off the lights, and call the day off.

All the above methods will help you conserve your willpower. Chose the methods you think will work the best for you and don't be afraid to mix and match, be creative and change them slightly to what makes sense to you.

When reaching for your goals, persistence is as important as willpower. Willpower is the basis of persistence, and in the next chapter I will analyze why persistence should be used as an important source of motivation.

CHAPTER 11

PERSISTENCE

*"Nothing in the world can take the place of persistence. Talent
will not; nothing is more common than unsuccessful men with
talent. Genius will not; unrewarded genius is almost a proverb.
Education alone will not; the world is full of educated derelicts.
Persistence and determination alone are omnipotent."* [1]

– John Calvin Coolidge Jr., 30th President of the United States

*"If you can't fly you run, if you can't run you walk, if you
can't walk you crawl. But no matter what, you keep moving
forward."* [2]

– Martin Luther King Jr., Leader in the African-American Civil
Rights Movement

*"Lack of persistence is one of the major causes of failure.
Moreover, experience with thousands of people has proved that
lack of persistence is a weakness common to the majority of
men. It is a weakness which may be overcome with effort."* [3]

– Napoleon Hill, Personal Success Author

Surveys indicate kids under 7 years old are "most persistent" to get what they want, more than any other age group. Anyone who has been around this age group will not be surprised to find this out. Kids will give you all the signals and will do whatever they can think of to get your attention and eventually to get their way. This may be by their tantrum, or crying – yet the results are the same. While people as kids are very persistent, when they get older they change their ways and become the opposite. They are ready to quit at the first obstacle and this, in most cases, results in failure.

Being patient and persistent in life, are probably the two most important qualities necessary to achieve success. Having a goal and plans are not enough. Mike Tyson put it well when he said, "Everyone's got a plan until they get punched in the face."[4]

These are a few good reasons why being persistent, patient, and well-prepared are very important to achieve your goals:

1. **Things don't usually go as planned:** While we are executing our plan, and as prepared as we may think we are, inevitable roadblocks may happen and we need to be ready to face them. The key is to remain focused on what lies ahead to foresee potential obstacles, and then adjust accordingly. Changing our plans (and often), may become necessary to achieve the desired success. We always have to have in mind though, that experiencing failures along our path to success doesn't mean we actually failed. Failing occurs when we let those experiences cause us to quit.

2. **Planning doesn't ensure adaptability:** A very basic

rule in the planning process is to "plan your work, and work your plan". Having a plan though doesn't ensure adaptability. A million things may happen that can affect our plan and unless we adapt, we will be unable to ensure its success. Persistence and patience will give us the strength and energy to make the necessary changes under the new environment and situations.

3. **Planning doesn't identify unknowns:** Planning will help us identify what we already know. It doesn't help us though to identify things we do not know, or things we are not aware of. When we come across those things that are out of our control, we need to stay positive and keep moving. Persistence and tenacity is what will make us successful.

4. **Good plans are worthless without execution:** Without a doubt, having a good plan (especially contingency plans) is extremely important. Having the intuition to foresee changes and adapt accordingly is important as well. While you may have spent all the time in the world to develop your plans and you have the intuition to see possible changes coming, if you do not take action and apply those plans, then your plans have zero value. In the end they are just ideas placed on a paper in a drawer that no one will ever hear about and you will never know if they had their chance to develop into something great. You need to take action, but also have the ability to execute your plans flawlessly. If you don't have the ability, and the persistence needed to stick to your plan, the probability is you will fail.

5. **Accept that failure happens:** When we are discouraged, we often believe we are the only ones who fail. The truth though is most successful people in life have all failed. Here are a few examples of people most of us know who have failed at some point in their life[5, 6, 7, 8]:

- Marilyn Monroe was booted from 20th Century-Fox, after producers declared her "unattractive."

- Oprah was fired from one of her early anchor gigs, after being labelled "unfit for TV."

- Walt Disney was fired by a newspaper editor because he "lacked imagination and had no good ideas."

- Steven Spielberg got rejected from film school ... three times!

- The Beatles were dropped by their record label.

- Thomas Edison's teachers told him he was "too stupid to learn anything."

- J.K. Rowling was a single mom living off welfare when she began writing the first "Harry Potter" novel.

- Vincent Van Gogh sold only one painting, "The Red Vineyard," in his life, and the sale was just months before his death.

- Lucille Ball appeared in so many second-tier films at the start of her career that she became known as "The Queen of B Movies."

The difference between them and people who live in fear of failure is successful people face the failure, learn from it, and use it to spur their next attempt. Whether or not we like it, failure happens. To thrive, you need to start seeing failure as part of achievement, and a natural part of the road to success.

Ask yourself:

- What is my attitude towards failure?

- Am I scared of failing?

- Am I avoiding failure by never persisting at anything?

- Am I willing to accept failure and see it as an opportunity to learn and laser focus to what matters?

Know things don't usually go as planned. Planning doesn't ensure adaptability and doesn't identify unknowns; good plans are worthless without execution, and failure happens. Then it is easier to accept that being persistent and patient is the natural path towards achievement.

Reasons that cause lack of persistence

Sometimes, not being persistence has its source, and we are simply not aware of it. These are some of the possible reasons:

- **We are not really inspired by our goal:** Very often, when we have so many choices of things to do, and goals to achieve, we are overwhelmed and we focus on goals that don't necessary inspire us. In addition, when we make the decision to pursue

119

a goal based on the fact we are excited or vulnerable, we do not take all the facts into consideration and we do not make a valid decision as to why we really want to go after that goal. In addition, many of us will not do what we really want, but what others expect from us. This type of behavior doesn't take us far. Regardless of the reason, we are entitled to change our opinion about pursuing a goal. Things change and once something does not inspire us any more, then it is a given our determination to achieve it will decrease.

- **We procrastinate:** Procrastination, the action of delaying or postponing something, is the enemy of persistence and the thief of your precious time. 95% of people procrastinate on their goals. Be different from them! To build the strength of persistence, it's important to a) identify the reasons that cause you to procrastinate and b) develop a plan as how to deal with them. These are some of the reasons that cause procrastination:

1) **Fear:** Our lack of persistence often is caused by fear. Fear has many forms including:

   a) The fear you are not good enough and the fear others will find out you are not good enough.

   b) The fear of an unsure outcome. You do not want to spend time and energy on something you are not sure is achievable.

   c) The fear of success. Success creates more obligations and responsibilities and you feel you are not going to be able to handle them, or maintain the level of success you achieved.

d) You are a perfectionist fearing by taking action you may show your flaws.

e) The fear of rejection. You are afraid of being rejected and do not want to face the pain you think you will feel if you are rejected.

2) **Feeling pressure to perform:** When we feel loss of control, we feel powerless and we feel pressure from others to perform; many times we resist; we become resentful and finally we end up procrastinating.

3) **Sense of entitlement:** The desire to achieve results quickly without much effort, and the sense of entitlement, often prevent us from taking action and being persistent.

4) **Learned helplessness:** This is a state of mind where we procrastinate because we may feel that no matter what we do, our actions will not make much of a difference.

While we all may have our reasons to procrastinate, after we identify those reasons, we need to develop a plan as to how to deal with them. What follows are some examples of possible reasons of procrastination and methods of action:

a) **Complex projects:** break the project down into smaller components and tackle each component individually.

b) **Unpleasant projects:** implement a reward system for completing an unpleasant task.

c) **Inability to prioritize:** make a list of your tasks and prioritize them based on urgency and importance. Then set a goal of completing a certain number of tasks (preferred top 3) in the next four hours. After four hours evaluate your progress and reassess the situation based on the remaining tasks.

d) **Inability to make decisions:** set up a plan where you are making daily small decisions for the purpose of practicing. After 3 weeks move to bigger decisions.

e) **Fear of failure:** visualize yourself achieving your goal and imagine the steps you will need to take to succeed. Then take action.

f) **Distractions and temptation:** set up your workspace in a way it helps you minimize distractions; plan your meetings in advance with coworkers, and anyone associated with your project. In your personal life minimize anything that can take you away from your goal (watching TV, spending a lot of time on social media, etc.)

When you have determined the underlying reasons that causes you lack of persistence, the next step is to design a 'persistence approach' to set you in forward motion. This calls for having a vision, turning problems into opportunities, and developing proactive beliefs and behaviors.

How does one develop persistence?

Persistence is a very important skill in the process of transforming desire into its final form, which is the realization of a goal.

When willpower, the basis of persistence, and desire are combined, they make a powerful pair. [9]

Persistence is a state of mind, some would say, skill; that can be cultivated. One can develop persistence by applying some, or all of the following approaches. The effect each approach may have depends on the individual, their goals, and their experiences:

1. **Change how you see yourself:** The most important trick for becoming more persistent is to trick your mind into believing you are a persistent person until it actually happens. We need to monitor our thinking, and when the urge to quit arises, the first and best response should be quitting is not part of who we are, and we are going to finish whatever we started. Thinking of the big picture will always help us stay in focus. [10]

2. **Define your Purpose:** What is defined by some as passion, your purpose is what keeps you awake at night due to excitement or fear of never having accomplished your goal or the fear of losing what you love. What do you really want the most? Do you want to launch a new product, take your business into a new market, or run a marathon? Record all the things you want to have or accomplish and be as specific as possible. List all your desires and wants, no matter how impossible they are to achieve at the moment. Then set milestones as to when you will accomplish them.

   Motivation comes from a deep reason why we want to achieve or have something. Knowing what we want can become a strong motive and the driving force to help us build persistence. Your purpose must be bigger than any obstacles that may occur. You can possibly find your purpose – your powerful reason to be and to do – by asking the following two questions: a) What is the most important thing in my life? b) What is the greatest fear in my life? The answers to those two questions helps you find your purpose.

3. **Desire:** Persistence is directly linked to our desire. When we want something bad enough we will develop the mindset and the high level of persistence needed to go after what we want and do whatever it takes to accomplish it. Possible obstacles seem very small when our desire is high enough and often we feel we can move mountains.

4. **Having a plan:** When we have developed an organized plan, it is easier to follow it through and persist than when we do not have plan where we do not know the starting point or ending point or where we are going. Even when our plans are weak, and difficult to accomplish, they still put us in a better position than not having a plan. Plans encourage persistence.

5. **Track Your Progress:** Keep a daily journal or check off progress on a calendar or computer. Refer back to the SMART goals you set and use them to keep you on track. Tracking your progress will show proof of your persistence and be rewarding to you. [11]

6. **Knowledge:** Knowledge based on experience, shared knowledge that comes from others we trust, and knowledge based on observation and studying encourage persistence. When, on the other hand, we do not have the knowledge and we are guessing at things, our persistence diminishes.

7. **Believing in ourselves:** When we believe we have the ability to execute a plan, we persist no matter what obstacles may come in front of us, and we do not let anything to stop us.

8. **Procrastination:** To build the strength of persistence, you need to identify the factors that are maintaining procrastination (example an unpleasant task) and develop a plan to tackle them.

9. **Building your Mastermind group:** A Mastermind group is composed of like-minded friends, colleagues, or mentors who can help you succeed towards your goal. You need to select these people very carefully as they will provide unbiased judgment, and will motivate you when your persistence is low. They should have a positive mental attitude, sympathize with you and each other, and be able to give you valuable lessons from their experiences so you don't need to find them yourself the hard way. Your Mastermind group should consist of people who are perfectly harmonized, whom you trust, and who look forward to learn from one other.

10. **Willpower:** Strong willpower develops persistence and helps you build, execute plans, and reach your goals.

11. **Develop habit and discipline:** The subconscious mind absorbs thoughts and images from the conscious mind and by repetition and autosuggestion they become habits. Persistence is the direct result of habit. If we want to develop persistence we need to develop habit. Developing habits can have huge benefits. For instance, fear, the worst of all enemies, can be effectively cured by forced repetition of acts of courage. [12]

Discipline, on the other hand, is the bridge between goals and accomplishments. By developing discipline, we can have the same positive results as when we develop good habits. Upholding discipline and good habits can help us stay on course, even despite difficulties.

12. **Use Small Wins to Establish a Habit of Persistence:** Small wins allow you to establish the habit of persistence. Establish everyday tasks and goals that result in small wins. Examples: Wake up early, exercise every day, finish your work always on time, etc. If you see persistence through small tasks as daily "wins", you will find it easier to persist through larger tasks. Especially if you start your day with a series of small wins, the pressure from the larger tasks will be removed and you will feel satisfied and accomplished.

13. **Use Daily Action to Establish a Habit of Persistence:** Persistence and taking action feed on each other. If you do not take action, then persistence is not necessary and if you do not persist in completing the goals and tasks you want, then you will not take action. Start small and use daily action to establish a habit of persistence. Develop a habit of taking consistent action on a daily basis and expand until you find yourself taking action in more areas of your life. Then, when life's problems tempt you to slow down, it will not seem foreign to continue taking action. Create a list of items you should do every day to help you develop your persistence. If you are a sales person, do cold calls every day, if you want to learn a foreign language read every day, if only for 15 minutes, and so on.

14. **Use reminders:** Reminders can help you build persistence.

Put reminders of the end goal, in prominent places. For example, if your goal is to buy a house, put a picture of your dream house on your bathroom mirror. [13]

15. **Avoid quitting at the first sign of difficulty:** Anything worth doing or achieving is going to encounter hurdles and difficulties. Be prepared to face those difficulties and avoid quitting at the first sign of things being difficult. Think always of the big picture, what motivates you, and the reward of accomplishing what you want. [14]

16. **Don't underestimate the amount of time required:** Instant success rarely happens. While most people understand it will take a lot of effort to achieve their goal, at the same time they underestimate the length of time it takes to get there. The journey to success is a marathon, not a sprint, so prepare yourself accordingly.

17. **Minimize your stress:** Stress can become a big obstacle as it prevents us from thinking clearly, performing to the best of our abilities, and focusing on the bigger picture. In addition, stress consumes a lot of our energy, which we need, especially to do difficult tasks. We need to learn to manage and minimize our stress if we want to stay on track and be aligned with our goal.

18. **Keep a positive mental attitude:** Focusing on performance goals, outcomes, and whether you succeed or fail can become very demotivating. [15] To develop persistence, and eventually succeed in your endeavor, always maintain a positive mental attitude, regardless of the situation. Accept roadblocks will happen, focus on the present, and be prepared to replace

those negative thoughts and fears with self-assurance and persistence on taking action towards your goals. Overall enjoy the process, and keep the perspective that it will all work out in the end – one way or another.

19. **Accept failure happens, and be prepared for obstacles and setbacks:** One of the main reasons people give up early is having wrong expectations. They expected the way to be easy and are surprised when they find the reality to be the opposite. Their enthusiasm quickly melts and they lose faith. The reality though is, even the most successful people in life, at some point failed. It is inevitable; obstacles and setbacks will happen until we achieve success. Thomas Edison is said to have tried 10,000 times to create the light bulb before he succeeded. His attitude was: "I have not failed. I've just found 10,000 ways that don't work." [16]

Successful people persist because they know failure is simply part of achievement. Since failure is a certainty on the path to success, knowing how to handle it is critical. By knowing how to handle failure you will be able to keep your persistence. On the other hand, not being able to handle it will soon drain your mental energy. [17]

One of the things you can do to prepare for setbacks and obstacles is to be mentally ready, anticipate potential problems, allow room for their existence, and have an emergency plan. Explore possible scenarios and create just-in-case plans to battle those obstacles. If you have a strict exercise program and one day you do not go to the gym for whatever reason, do not beat yourself up. Be ok with it, and make a new agreement with yourself to cover the lost time. For example, you can go to the gym the next day for two hours instead of the usual one hour. Most importantly, remember encountering problems does not mean you have failed and this should not be the reason to quit. All you have to do is revise your plans and repeat your efforts.

20. **Maintain focus and keep the end in mind:** Sometimes we pay so much attention to the small tasks and the things we do not want to do, we lose sight of the big picture and what we really want to accomplish. This is where we need to regain our focus and our motivation and think what persisting to the end will do to us. If the reward is big enough, we can stay on task when the difficulties become discouraging.

A good way to maintain focus is to visualize yourself accomplishing your goal no matter what; avoid getting caught up in negative or unproductive thinking such as, "This will never work." "I can't do this." Instead, keep inspiring slogans handy, pictures of those who have persevered in life, and whatever else will motivate, boost your drive and keep your persistence alive. [18]

21. **Model Someone Successful:** Understanding successful people need persistence to achieve success will inspire you to be persistent yourself. Chances are you are not the first person to have gone through the process you are going through. So find and read life stories of successful people in history. Study the example they have set for you and use them as daily motivation. Hang their pictures and quotations around home and work to remind you constantly of what it takes to persist in the face of adversity.

22. **Take the first step and capitalize on the momentum:** Sometimes getting started is the hardest part. This can be all too true when your project requires a day-in day-out operation. You cannot persevere; much less succeed, if you never try to accomplish something. So many of us procrastinate, fear failure, or are too frozen in our tracks to take the first step towards achievement. [19] You will not fail if you don't try something, however, you will never succeed either. A good way to start something is by practicing the 5 minute technique. Commit you will spend only five minutes to do the required task. Usually you will end up doing much more than needed, and the rest will take care of itself.

23. **Rest, then Start Again:** When we are working on a big project, it's impossible to go all out all the time. At times we need to retreat and take a purposeful down period to renew our energy and passion. By doing this we will come back more enthusiastic about our goal and we will get better results than if we kept going without a break. Another good idea is to follow the run-walk technique. Alternating periods of intense effort with moderate effort can keep us going longer. The method applies in other areas of our life too; we do not have to apply it only when we want to cultivate persistence. We can go farther if we take breaks, go easy, relax, and rejuvenate.

24. **Be Persistent while Enjoying the Journey:** You must be persistent while also enjoying the journey from conceiving your idea and what you would like to do, to goal accomplishment. The greatest feelings of accomplishment originate from knowing you've overcome obstacles and conquered adversities to achieve your goals. Your ultimate

success will be much more satisfying and fulfilling when you know what it took to get there.

25. **Kill the distractions:** Remove the unimportant stuff that works against your determination and wears down the will to accomplish what you really want. How many hobbies, activities, meetings, projects, even relationships are making it impossible to keep up our determination when it matters most?

26. **Persist everywhere:** Everything you do in your life should be aligned with your goals. What you feed your body, soul, and mind should be interconnected and build each other up. You cannot expect to become an Olympic athlete if you do not eat properly, if you have a life style with bad habits, if you do not push your body to its limits and mentally believe you can't do it. Persistence should be present in every field of your life, not only one.

27. **Use the "broken record technique":** When people try to test your persistence, use the "broken record technique". This technique is based in assertiveness training and the main concept is simple. When the person you're interacting with keeps trying to redirect you elsewhere, you keep on repeating a clear and reasonable refusal or request. Basically, this technique consists of making a continuous, clear statement about your feeling, intention, or decision without becoming angry, defensive, or irritated, no matter how much you have to repeat yourself.

Persistence is an important part of life. Without persistence we leave things unfinished, we do not accomplish our goals, and we end up having regrets for not achieving our dreams. When you have persistence, it pays off in the long-term. Just recall, most successful people have failed at least once. Eventually though they succeeded because they had persistence.

Here are 5 reasons why having persistence pays off:

1. Most successful people fail at least once or more before succeeding.

2. People like to test you on persistence, so be ready when it happens.

3. What comes to you easily probably is not worthwhile.

4. Knowledge isn't gained without persistence.

5. The more you apply something, the easier it gets.

Before you move to another chapter, evaluate yourself and how persistent you think you are. Be honest with yourself, ask simple questions and try to determine if there are any fields in your life where you lack persistence, and identify the reasons for not having persistence. Then develop a plan as to what you intend to do to develop and maintain your persistence.

CHAPTER 12

HAPPINESS AND GRATITUDE

When we are not happy, we often feel unmotivated to go after our goals or the things we need to accomplish which are important to us. Increasing our levels of happiness is an important step towards our mission to achieve our goals, and an important tool we can use to increase our motivation. The happier we are, the more motivated we feel to do things to maintain and increase our levels of happiness. When something feels "nice", we want more of the same feeling and this motivate us to go after all the things that recreate the same feeling.

However, we all have different ideas as to what happiness is, and how to get it. What follows are some of the things you can do to increase your happiness and eventually your motivation. As everyone is different not everything may apply to everyone. While the following are some suggestions, think of the things YOU know make you happy and use them as a guide to increase your motivation:

1. **Exercise your way to happiness:** Exercise can help you to relax, increase your brain power, improve your body image and the way you feel about yourself. Exercise has a deep effect on our happiness, and it's been proven to be an effective strategy for overcoming depression. Exercising even seven minutes a day, may be enough to increase and maintain happiness. [1]

2. **Have sufficient quality sleep:** Sleeping more lets you be less sensitive to negative emotions. The quality and the length of your sleep affects how you feel when you wake up; this can make a difference to your whole day. [2]

3. **Cut down traveling time to work:** Studies have shown a long commute to work is something that can affect us dramatically, especially when we are driving in heavy traffic, and if we have been doing this for a long period of time. Move closer to your job, or chose to work for a company located within 30 minutes distance from your home. [3]

4. **Have 10 good friends; spend time with them and your family:** Surveys have shown we need at least 10 good friends (this may include family members) before we can reach the minimum "happy" level. We are happier when we have family and friends and many of the things we do, are just ways of getting more family and friends.

   On the other hand, as it takes time to maintain those close relationships, we may end up having a lot of people around us and still feel unhappy. It all comes down to the amount of time, and the quality of time, we spend with the people that matters to us the most. Increasing the strength of our social relationships is very important to reach happiness, and not spending enough time with the people we care about, can be one of our biggest regrets in life.

5. **Spend time outside:** Spending 20 minutes outside, on a nice sunny day, can increase positive mood, broaden thinking, and improve working memory. Your happiness is maximized

at 13.9°C, but any comfortable sunny day will make you feel happier. [4]

6. **Help others and practice kindness:** Volunteering for a cause you believe in is rewarding in terms of higher life satisfaction. Two hours a week significantly increases our levels of happiness; spending money on other people makes us happier than buying stuff for ourselves. Helping others, whether you do it directly or anonymously, actually makes the helpers happier. [5]

7. **Smile! Smiling relieves stress and anxiety:** Smiling, when we back it with positive thoughts, relieves stress and anxiety, alleviates some of the pain we feel in troubling circumstances, improves our attention and helps us perform better on cognitive tasks.

   Practice smiling and you will see a big difference in the way you feel. [6]

8. **Plan a vacation or just time away from work:** Use your Calendar as a tool and make plans for a trip, even if you cannot take it right away and it is months ahead. Making holiday plans, and plans to spend time away from work, can boost your levels of happiness.

9. **Meditate and live a happier life:** Meditation increases positive emotion, clears your mind, calms you down, and may decrease anxiety, depression and stress. Meditation has been often shown to be the single most effective way to live a happier live. [7]

10. **Practice mindfulness in what you are doing:** Mindfulness is a mental state achieved by focusing one's awareness on the present moment, while calmly acknowledging and accepting one's feelings, thoughts, and bodily sensations. Do it while working or playing; set deliberate time aside to be mindful and always couple it with the deep breathing we've talked about in other chapters.

    Being aware of what you are doing and just being present may increase your happiness significantly. When your mind wanders, you day dream, and you are unable to focus on what you are doing; you can feel less happy. [8]

11. **Spend time with happy people:** Happiness is contagious and our happiness is partially affected by our social network (not the Facebook kind). Knowing and spending quality time with happy people will have a positive effect on your life, will improve your mood, and increase your positive thinking. [9]

12. **Act like an extrovert:** Extroverts are generally happier, studies show. In addition, introverts feel happier when they act extroverted.

13. **Get a pet:** Unless you are using a pet to substitute for the lack of social life and/or the level of your commitment for taking care of a pet and understanding the responsibilities is low, then becoming a pet owner will bring you a great amount of happiness, pleasure and fun.

14. **Have fun:** Choosing fun activities where you participate with your whole self; losing yourself and forgetting everything else, can make you happy.

15. **Embrace failure:** Failing in work, love, and life can bring happiness, if we chose to learn from our mistakes.

16. **Buy experiences and stuff that creates experiences:** Tickets to sport events, concerts, or the theatre to share with your family or friends, or things that create experiences (example a membership in a flying club) are the kind of purchases that can make you happy.

17. **Engage in control-based activities:** Happiness and having control are two things that are interconnected and affect each other. This means if you take away somebody's control, they are less happy. At the same time if you give them more control they are generally happier, and more motivated to do something. This is one of the main reasons why there are so many people in the world who like to be in control, and it's the reason video games have become so popular. Some control-based activities you may want to try are:

    • Playing chess

    • Reading

    • Writing

    • Hiking (primarily alone)

    • Video Games

18. **Be optimistic:** Recollect a time where perhaps you went to friend's wedding, you had an exceptionally happy day; then the next day you went back to your home and to your old

settled routine. This is an example of an event that can bring us a lot of happiness, yet eventually we return to what is the norm for us. Good or bad events affect our happiness temporarily and eventually happiness tends to quickly revert to the baseline level. By being optimistic we maintain high level of happiness most of the time.

These are a few things you can do to maintain your optimism:

1) Start seeing the glass half full instead of half empty.

2) Be grateful; appreciate everything you already have. Include everything we take for granted and often do not appreciate. This may include the people in our life, food on our table, and even the clean water we drink.

3) Keep a journal and write down all the amazing little things happening in your day. Every day we accomplish little victories (yes, you did manage to wake up early and go to the gym before work. That IS victory!), and we all have those special joyful moments that energize us and keep us going. Think of a minimum of five things every day and write those things down.

4) Set yourself up for success, put yourself in situations where fortunate things are likely to be achieved or happen, where preparation meets opportunity. For example, if you prepare well for a test, most likely you will perform well during that test. On the contrary, if you cheat during a test, you set yourself for failure and you may have to face the consequences.

19. **Realize that fun is not happiness:** Happiness is what stays with us while fun is temporary and can be gone just as quickly.

20. **Own yourself:** Accept yourself exactly the way you are – including your habits, personality, the way you look and talk, your voice and everything else that makes you special and who you are. Believe in yourself, be comfortable in your own skin and don't try to change for anyone. Remember there is always someone who likes and appreciates you exactly the way you are.

21. **Have deep meaningful conversations:** Deep meaningful conversations, where we share our thoughts and ideas openly, not only helps us connect better and brings us closer to the people we are talking to, but can also increase our happiness. A study by a psychologist, Dr. S. Vazire, at Washington University in St. Louis has shown exactly that. Spending less time participating in small talk, and more time in deep, meaningful conversations eventually increases happiness. [10]

22. **Assess yourself:** Understanding that needs, goals, and desires change over time, figure out the big picture and what you really want in life at this specific phase of your life. Do you want to focus on your career? Do you want to improve your financial situation? Do you want to further your education? Are you tired of the single life and want to have a family? Decide whatever that might be, and record your individual clear short, medium, and long-term goals. Then plan your work, and work your plan. This means you need to plan step-by-step how you are going to achieve your goal, and then you need to take all the necessary actions to follow

that plan. Good planning is extremely important. When you have thought through most of the important steps you will save a lot of time thinking, questioning yourself, and you focus only on the things that matter. Eventually when you achieve your goal, you can restart by focusing on a new goal and developing a new plan.

23. **Follow the path of "cause and effect":** This simply means you need to look at what long-term results you may have caused as a result of your decisions and actions. If your goals are the cause, then what effects may those goals have had in your life? If as an example, your goal is to raise a family and have many children, then you may not have enough time to focus on your career. This doesn't necessarily mean you cannot be successful in both. The idea though is it is probable you will be more successful in one field than the other. For that reason, it is important to find the things you really want to do and you believe will make you happy.

24. **Make just enough money to meet the basic needs; then focus on time, not money:** There is the misconception by many people that money brings happiness. That is not necessarily the truth. Money buys us the ability to do the things we want to do, but it doesn't necessarily mean we will be happier. Once you make enough to support basic needs, your happiness is not significantly affected by how much money you make, but by your level of optimism, the quality of your relationships, the way you view life, your commitment to personal growth and so many other factors.

What significantly increases your happiness is the amount of available time you have to do things you want. Time is precious; it cannot be manufactured. When people realize how precious time is, they value it more and are more focused about how they use time – which makes them happier.

25. **Treat your body like it deserves to be happy:** Researchers have found exercise, healthy diets, and regular sleep to be key factors in growing happier and staying that way.

   a. **Exercise:** Regular exercise is associated with improved mental well-being and a lower incidence of depression. Further, physically active people have higher incidences of enthusiasm and excitement.

   b. **Healthy diets:** Fruits and vegetables, lean meats and proteins, whole grains, nuts, and seeds — give your body and brain the energy it needs to be healthy. On the contrary, unhealthy diets can cause long-lasting negative effects to your body and brain.

   c. **Get enough sleep:** Studies have confirmed sleep is key to happiness and peak performance. The more you sleep, the happier you tend to be. A very interesting study done by the University of Michigan, revealed getting just a little more sleep had a greater effect on a person's state of mind than a large increase in income. According to psychology professor Norbert Schwarz, one of the authors of the study, "Making $60,000 more in annual income has less of an effect on your daily happiness than getting one extra hour of sleep a night." If you're middle-aged, shoot to get at least eight hours of sleep per night; [11] the young and elderly should try to get 9 to 11 hours of sleep per night.

26. **Find happiness in the kind of work you have now:** Many believe if they find a new job or change their career, will drastically increase their levels of happiness. On the contrary, someone's positive outlook in life and the quality of relationships they maintain, surpass the satisfaction gained from work.

   People with a positive outlook in life, can make the best out of the worst situation; they will see opportunities, and find things to be happy even in a job they do not like. Overall, the contribution of a job to someone's happiness is quite small when compared to the outlook of life and meaningful relationships. Actually, the satisfaction from meaningful relationships will fulfill you regardless of the kind of job you do.

   This doesn't mean you shouldn't be motivated to find a job which potentially makes you happier; after all you spend at least 8 hours a day at work.

27. **Forgive:** Studies have shown forgiveness can make you happier and healthier. Forgiveness can reduce stress, anxiety, and depression and helps you let go of anger and hatred; it helps you sleep better and gives you peace and more energy for fun. In addition, being able to overcome an issue through forgiveness opens you up to a world of positive communication and keeps you from feeling repressed. Forgiveness also increases confidence; it reduces blood pressure and heart rate and can boost your immune system. A 2011 Duke University study showed positive immune system changes in those living with HIV who forgave someone in their lives. Researchers theorized based on the evidence that

higher levels of forgiveness increased the percentage of CD4 cells, which play a positive role in the immune system.

28. **Monitor your habits and what may affect your happiness:** Become aware of your habits as they may affect your happiness. People who spend too much time on social media rather than interacting with people around them, tend to be less happy. Another example is the habit of people checking their email all the time. People who check their email at a few set times during the day are less stressed than people who constantly check their email.

Spread Happiness and Give off Positive Energy

While it's important to be happy yourself, it is as important to spread happiness to other people and give off positive energy. These are some of the things you can do to accomplish that [12]:

1. **Smile and engage:** Make it a habit to smile, engage, and genuinely care about what others say. Being friendly, compassionate, and thoughtful you are able to give away positive energy and make others feel good.

2. **Make happiness a priority:** Happiness is contagious and you can only give away positive energy when you are happy yourself. Make happiness a priority for yourself and this will eventually be passed to others.

3. **Love and appreciate yourself, others, and everything around you:** Loving yourself, being appreciative for everything you have in your life, and passing love and gratitude to others is a great way to spread happiness and positive energy.

4. **Say more positive words:** Our language, and the words we use when we interact with other people, can have a significant impact in spreading happiness. Use positive words that touch, move, and inspire others and show your appreciation for having those people in your life. Don't be afraid to say "Thank you", and "I love you", to the people who matter to you.

Practice Gratitude

You can do many things to increase happiness, but the one thing you can do that stands out the most, and can make a huge difference on your outlook in life, is to practice gratitude.

What is gratitude though?

Gratitude is a feeling or attitude in acknowledgment of a benefit one has received or will receive. By practicing gratitude you will increase both happiness and life satisfaction. [13] Very often we are so focused on the things we want to accomplish we just take for granted or completely ignore everything we already have. Practicing gratitude can be a great tool to help us change all those negative thoughts and self-doubt into positive thoughts and help us focus on the future and the things we want to accomplish.

You need to start appreciating and being thankful for everything in your life you already have. [14] By acknowledging and appreciating what you do have, you can combat the feeling of being incomplete and unsatisfied and not having enough of something whether that is money, time, friends, emotional validation, etc. Appreciate your family, your job (even if you do not like it – if you do not have a job appreciate the free time you have to do the things you want), your friends, skills and talents, your imperfections that make you unique, the fact you can see, you can walk, your overall health, and that you are alive. Lyrics from a Pitbull [15] song say, "every day above ground is a great day". Although the subject is gloomy, these words always give me a different perspective about the things I need to appreciate. Even though you may think there are many things going wrong in your life there is always going to be a plethora of things you can be grateful for including: the air you breath and the water you drink, nature and the beauty that surround us, the people who love you and appreciate you for who you are, other people's kindness, a great sunny day, and so many things.

Practicing gratitude on a daily basis puts you in a great state of mind and helps you have a positive perspective on life. Wake up every morning and go to sleep every night feeling grateful. Unconditionally love life and all it has to offer; do your best to see beauty in everything. Appreciate the little things that happen within the day such as the compliments you receive, encouragement from others, or a kind word. Here are some of things you can do to **cultivate gratitude**:

1) **Keep a gratitude journal:** For this very effective practice, get a journal, and record regularly the things you are really grateful for. The best approach would be to start each day by writing those things down. Even though you may repeat some things over a long period of time, always remember you have many things to be grateful for; all you need to do is discover them. Doing this, will put you in a more positive, empowering frame of mind. [16]

2) **Gratitude Letter & Visit – Thank You Messages and Notes:** Another very powerful gratitude practice is to think of someone who has had a significant impact on your life, write a letter of gratitude, and then visit and read it to them in person. "Gratitude is the heart's memory," says a French proverb [17]. Therefore, one of the first steps to thankfulness is to remember those in our lives who have walked with us and shown kindness for deeds big and small. In addition, say thank you often or send thank you messages and notes to the ones that matter most to you. You do not have to have a reason to thank others at a specific moment. Just because you felt it, and you want to show your appreciation is a good enough reason. [18]

3) **Appreciate the present moment:** Practice Mindfulness to appreciate the present moment and experience what is right in front of you. Use all of your senses; allow yourself to feel, hear, smell, see, and taste. This practice gives you a different perspective and appreciation of things that surround you.

4) **Acknowledge and replace ungrateful thoughts:** Learning to hear, question, and alter your thoughts into something more grateful is truly a blessing, for it gives you the power to change your life. Practice replacing every day ungrateful thoughts, bad emotions when you are in a difficult situation, complaints, criticism, and gossip with appreciation. [19]

5) **Compliment others:** Genuinely compliment others or ask someone to share your appreciation for something (example: I'm so grateful we have a great sunny day).

6) **Sound genuinely happy:** When you meet in person, talk with people on the phone, or chat with them online, focus on the moment and sound genuinely happy to be in contact with them. When you sound happy, they will know you value your time with them.

7) **Volunteer:** Become involved in a cause that is important to you. By joining the cause and donating money or your time or your talent you'll gain greater appreciation for the organization, and you will show your gratitude.

8) **Use Positive Words:** Positive words propel the motivational centers of the brain into action and build resiliency. Use words that make you happy – that are positive and exciting. You can start your day by saying "I will have an amazing empowering day", rather than saying "I know my day will suck". Negative and disempowering words create negative feelings and bring negative results.

CHAPTER 13

THE POWER OF LOVE

"One word frees us of all the weight and pain of life: That word is love." [1]

– Sophocles, Ancient Greek Tragedian

When you have a purpose, and you are "in love" with your purpose, you are able to do things you never before thought were possible. Take as an example someone who is in love with another person. They have a great amount of energy throughout the day and night; they are vibrant, radiant, beaming and they are glowing. You can actually see, at some level, their aura when they come into a room. They have an asserted confidence and they walk differently, they talk differently, they are happy and you can tell, even if you are on the other side of the room that this person is either in love or about to fall in love.

On the other hand, if the same person loses their love interest, their energy level falls drastically, they lose interest in life; in many cases they can hardly move.

How, can the same person go from feeling they can move mountains to actually having so little energy that they can hardly move? The answer is love.

Love is energy and a power that motivates us to do things for ourselves and others without seeing obstacles or limitations. You need to harvest the power of love, use it as a motivation tool and let it guide you to achieve the things you have always wanted.

First, you have to genuinely fall in love with life. Appreciate truly everything life has to offer and make it your personal goal to live a passionate and exciting life and make every day special.

As you learn to love life, allow yourself to fall in love with people – not necessarily lovers – and appreciate them for who they are, without trying to change them to meet your own standards. Be there for the people you love, support them, and stand up for them and what they believe in. Volunteer in your communities and help the ones who are less fortunate than you. Support a cause that inspires you, by offering your time and money, even if you do not have any personal connection with that cause. Be generous, live by example, and inspire others with your positive outlook on life.

Fall in love with nature, animals, any form of life, and the wonderful world that surrounds us. Don't take nature for granted, but enjoy it and protect it. A simple act, like going for a walk in the park, and by just being present and living in that moment, may give you the opportunity to notice all the little miracles around you, a better understanding of life, and help you get the answers you have been looking for, for your own purpose and goals. After all, we are all connected and if we allow it, nature and animals can become our greatest teachers. If you ever think you do not have "courage", it is "not possible" and "you can't", you may want to consider little birds that fly every autumn thousands of miles, many times above ocean to avoid cold winters.

Love yourself and your body exactly the way you are, as you are absolutely perfect; do not allow anyone to tell you otherwise. Humans are by nature social animals and often in our effort to be accepted, we try to change who we are to get the approval of others. There is never a guarantee though we will ever get others' approval, as much as we may try, and as many drastic measures we may take. Our mistake is instead of acknowledging everything that is good about us including our personality, body, skills, knowledge, and experiences and moving forward, we often focus on the things we "think", others may not like. We "hide" parts of our personality or even we hide physically, in the fear we will not be accepted, when all that happens is we miss opportunities to be discovered. For others to love you, you need to start loving yourself, even with the imperfections you may think you have. You are the way you are for a reason, you are unique and you need to embrace that. This does not mean you should stop seeking improvement, excellence, and to better yourself at every opportunity.

As you increase your levels of love and awareness – now is the time to fall deeply and passionately in love with your "project". This may be building a business, losing weight, travelling to a place you always wanted to go, or any other goals you are going after.

What is it you want to accomplish? Write it down and fall in love with it.

Your goal should consume your mind, it should drive you to the point you are absolutely obsessed with it, and you should be eager to spend all the necessary time needed to make it happen and form in reality. The deeper you fall in love with your goal/project, the more energy it will get and your love for it will grow. Ideas that will support your goal will flow and your determination will increase. As your love for your goal grows, you will realize you will be eager to stand up and defend it no matter what – this is something you absolutely need to do regardless. And as your commitment grows, you need to remember you should not be attached to the final result. Appreciate any results you are getting – positive or negative – and acknowledge the effort you are giving.

In case your project/goal involves others (such as a business venture), don't suffocate it with your love, but instead you should give it the opportunity to grow and reach its full potential by seeking advice from others when needed, accept help when offered, and let others lead it when you feel their skills, knowledge, and talents will place it in a better, competitive position in the business world. Let others fall in love with your goal/purpose, as much as you are.

As you are moving forward remember love is a power that:

- **Gives you energy:** you may find you wake up earlier and have the energy to accomplish more within the day for yourself and others, in less time. [2]

- **Enhances your creativity:** your love, and determination to have or accomplish what inspires you, will motivate you to think of creative solutions to issues or think of alternative ways of accomplishing your goal.

- **Helps you grow:** the love for others, a project or a goal helps us push ourselves to our limits and ultimately expand and grow.

- **Makes you feel better:** even if you're in perfect health, love makes you feel better emotionally and physically. If you are dealing with any physical issues, love can give you the motivation and positive energy to heal faster.

- **Makes you feel validated:** giving or receiving love from others often gives people validation, security that others believe in them, a purpose, and an appreciation of how much their life matters. Love reminds us we are not all alone and we have each other to support in life.

- **Makes you want to do nice things for others:** when you are "in love", you are more generous and want to do great things for people in your life who are important to you and those in need; you want to share that wonderful feeling.

Make it a priority and share positive energy and love on a daily basis. There are a few simple things you can do:

1. Smile and engage (talk to others even if you do not feel like it)

2. Make happiness a priority (by being happy, you can pass this to others)

3. Be loving and grateful for all the great things happening in your life

4. Say positive words (I love, thank you)

5. Do something that energizes you and makes you happy (sport, singing, traveling, spending time with the people you love)

CHAPTER 14

TAKING CARE OF YOUR BODY

"Νοῦς ὑγιὴς ἐν σώματι ὑγιεῖ".[1]

– Thales, pre-Socratic Greek Philosopher (Miletus, 624 – 546 BC)

'A sound mind in a sound body' is the English translation of a famous quotation by the pre-Socratic Greek philosopher, Thales, demonstrating the close links between physical exercise, mental equilibrium, and the ability to enjoy life.

What it means is when the body is kept in good condition, the mind works well and vice versa. When the brain functions well, then the body is also healthy.

Ancient Greece, Sparta, and Athens had a culture of sport – Athens adding in an emphasis on mind. Plato, a philosopher, and mathematician in Classical Greece felt the educational ideal was to strive for a balance and harmony between body and soul; Socrates famously said "It is a shame for a man to grow old without seeing the beauty and strength of which his body is capable."

Ancient Greeks could see a definite connection between a healthy body and a health mind; recently, many studies have shown the exact same thing.

So how does having a healthy body does help our mind?

- **Positive outlook:** Staying physically fit, coupled with eating healthy, is an important foundation for a positive outlook as it is harder to feel positive when you are unwell and/or unfit. Exercise has a profound effect on our happiness and well-being, and can help us relax and even improve our body image.

- **Helps the body and mind wake up and oxygenate:** Highly successful people know getting the body active is imperative on Monday mornings and through the week. Exercise helps body and mind wake up and oxygenate; by doing so, all of the cells become active and ready for the day. [2]

- **Keeping the mind sharp:** Physical exercise is known to keep the mind sharp. American president, Barack Obama shared with WebMD, "The rest of my time will be more productive if you give me my workout time." [3]

- **Improve circulation:** Physical exercise helps the brain by improving circulation and memory; balance, coordination, and reflexes. [4]

- **Physical exercise helps the brain:** Increasing the flow of blood delivers vital oxygen and glucose to the brain. The Franklin Institute says, physical exercise has been shown to stimulate the growth of cerebral blood vessels. [5]

- **Improved mood:** Physical exercise helps improve your mood because it increases the production of critical neurotransmitters found in the brain associated with good health and mental well-being. By increasing neurotransmitter levels, exercise works as a natural antidepressant. Physical exercise also helps to reduce stress levels and anxiety. [6]

- **Improve learning and memory:** Even moderate physical exercise, like walking, can boost memory functions, learning, and abstract reasoning. [7]

- **Increase brain power – more brain cells:** A 1999 Salk Institute study showed the adult human brain is capable of producing new cells. This process is called neurogenesis. Recent studies are showing physical exercise increases the brain's ability to grow new cells, and the more one exercises, the more new brain cells you can grow. [8]

- **Disease prevention (Alzheimer's):** According to the National Institutes of Health in the States, being physically active may help delay or even prevent the loss of cognitive function associated with age and disease. People who don't take any form of physical exercise are twice more likely than active people to develop diseases such as Alzheimer's. Exercise seems to slow or reverse the brain's physical decay, much as it does with muscles.

Research shows those who engage in regular physical activity have **better cognitive performance and more sustained attention spans than those with a sedentary lifestyle:** Exercise in conjunction with brain fitness (example: ballroom dancing) increases your chances of increasing cognitive functions, as the best brain health workouts involve those that integrate different parts of the brain such as coordination, rhythm, and strategy.

Our bodies are miracles and it is extremely important to take care of your body as much as it is to take care of your mind. Love yourself and your body the way it is and nurture it with healthy food, good sleep, a lot of rest, and exercise. Drink a lot of water, join a gym, or just walk. Educate yourself about the miracle your body is and how to protect it. If all you can do is walk, then just do that, and avoid consuming anything that can hurt you like drinking a lot of alcohol. Since a healthy mind equals a healthy body, make taking care of your body a part of your daily plan towards accomplishing your goals.

These are some of the things you can do to start immediately:

1) **Exercise more – 7 minutes might be enough.** Go for a walk in the park. Get a dog, go to the gym, or work out in the house while you are doing another activity such as watching a movie or the news. This way the mind will be focused on something else and you will not think of the physical exercise.

2) **Sleep more.** Sleep helps us rest and re-energize, reduces negative emotions, and increases happiness. How well and how long you sleep, affects how you feel when you wake up, making a big difference to your day.

3) **Eat healthy.** Eat foods that give you the nutrients you need to maintain your health, feel good, and have energy. These include protein, carbohydrates, fat, water, vitamins, and minerals. Healthy nutrition is very important for everyone. [9]

4) **Meditate and practice breathing techniques.** Take 7 deep breaths in, hold for four seconds, taking 7 deep breaths

out. Repeat first by inhaling through the nose and exhaling through the mouth, then use only your mouth.

5) **Drink a lot of water.** More than 90% of our body is water, so it is very important to stay hydrated. Drink a minimum of 8 glasses of water a day. [10]

CHAPTER 15

TAKE ACTION

"It is better, by noble boldness, to run the risk of being subject to half the evils we anticipate than remain in cowardly listlessness for fear of what might happen." [1]

– Herodotus, Greek Historian

"Do it now! can affect every phase of your life. It can help you do the things you should do but don't feel like doing. It can keep you from procrastinating when an unpleasant duty faces you. But it can also help you do those things that you want to do. It helps you seize those precious moments that, if lost, may never be retrieved." [2]

– Napoleon Hill, Personal Success Author

"Do not wait; the time will never be "just right." Start where you stand, and work with whatever tools you may have at your command, and better tools will be found as you go along." [3]

– Napoleon Hill, Personal Success Author

We all have goals we want to accomplish, but what really holds us back is we do not take action. In most cases, we even know exactly what needs to be done to get what we want – still we chose not to do anything. We want to lose weight, but we don't do anything about it. We want to gain knowledge, but we do not read books. We want a great body, but we chose not to exercise. Of course, we validate ourselves by giving ourselves reasons why we do not do things. "I cannot read a book because I do not have free time". Yet, during our lunch breaks, we spend time browsing social media. "I cannot stop smoking", yet we are the ones buying cigarettes. We always find reasons and excuses as to why we do not do things, yet we do not realize those reasons are not real, and they are creations of our minds. How many times have you said I cannot do it, it cannot happen, and then the solution comes to your mind? Anything is possible as long as we take action and we put our mind into it.

The main difference between successful and unsuccessful people is successful people have the habit of doing the things unsuccessful people don't want to do. When we do not take action on something right away, that 'something' becomes guilt and stays always at the back of our mind. We carry it with us when we go to sleep and it is with us when we wake up first thing in the morning. If we do not take action on the things we want, in the long-term we live in a vicious circle where our wishes and desires eat us up constantly, and then after years we regret all the opportunities we missed and the time we lost.

Taking action is extremely important. There is a huge difference between thinking of doing something and actually doing it. There is also a huge difference between thinking you are going to do something tomorrow and doing it today. Start now, even if you just take baby steps. Doing things little by little will take you where you want to be and help you reach your big goal. Registering at the gym, even if you don't go today, is a form of commitment and action. Don't wait and allow reasons and excuses stop you. Be committed to take action; don't procrastinate.

The most important word to remember is the word "NOW". You need to take action "now", even if it is a very small step towards your goal. If as an example, you want to start going to the gym, the simplest thing you can do is to book in your calendar a date and time where you will go and register. That's it. That is all you need to do and it will take you less than a minute. The next step is to follow through with your commitment and do what you said you will do.

These are some of the things you can do to make sure things are done and will support you in taking action:

a) Take one action right away. Do it the minute it comes to your mind. This can be something simple like putting it in your calendar or making a phone call to make a commitment. Procrastination is the biggest thing between us and getting what we want; by taking action right away we fight this enemy.

b) Make the commitment. If you want to take a class starting in 3 months, don't wait for the last minute; register now. Pay in advance for those music lessons. Splurge on a gym membership or personal trainer. When you make it inconvenient to back out, you increase the likelihood of following through.

c) Have something at stake. As an example give a substantial deposit to join a class. If you do not follow through, you will lose your money. This is an example of having something at stake.

d) Announce to others what you are planning to do. If you want to lose weight, call ten of your best friends and tell them you are planning to lose say 20 pounds within 4 months. Announcing this will hold you accountable and you will make sure you follow through to maintain your integrity. The bigger the announcement, the more committed you will be. [4]

e) Change your language. Every time you want to take action on something you want to do, but reasons and excuses come to your mind, replace the word "but" with the word "and". For example: "I want to go to the gym but I do not have time." changes to "I want to go to the gym AND I have time". This is simple, yet powerful, trick gives you a different perspective on things.

f) Use tools that help you towards taking action like your calendar, email reminders, computer, etc. I recommend you make your calendar your boss. When you plan ahead, you do not have to worry or think about it, you just follow your calendar. This is a good way of making sure things are happening.

g) The key to being unstoppable is to be unreasonable with ourselves and others. Powerful people are unreasonable with their own self and others and make unreasonable requests. We often use our reasons that stop us from making demands on ourselves and others. We need to change our mindset and every day take a new action, and make an unreasonable request related to the goal we want to accomplish. We have to remember when people say NO, they do not say no to us, but they say no to the request. If we take things personally, then we shut down the possibility of who we are.

h) Taking action and what other people think. Often we do not take action to do something, not because we are procrastinating or we do not have the means to do what we want, but because we worry what other people may think of us. If people say something that is not in alignment with what we want, or may offend us or invalidate us, and we let it affect us, then they are in full control of us. The actual price we pay is the freedom to do what we really want and to express ourselves. We have the freedom by doing exactly what we want, even though some people may not like it. There is **no guarantee** of the admiration of other people, so we might as well have integrity and go after what we want. Having integrity will give us the opportunity to be respected as someone who takes chances and lives life exactly the way we want.

Sometimes people who love us may not support us because they do not want to lose us. They want us to go after bigger and better things but they cannot adjust to the idea we may not be available for them as they would like us to be. They will have to adapt to our absence and they do not want to do that. They don't want us to leave; in some cases we will not win unless we make drastic changes.

As you move forward, the conditions and your environment change. When you adapt to the change, this gives you the ability to see the next step of action that is necessary. Use your time wisely and always take action in the present moment. You have one life to live, so get the most out of it, while accomplishing goals, celebrating your victories, enjoying and having fun.

CHAPTER 16

DEVELOPING A PLAN

"Create a definite plan for carrying out your desire and begin at once, whether you're ready or not, to put this plan into action." [1]

– Napoleon Hill, Personal Success Author

"If you don't design your own life plan, chances are you'll fall into someone else's plan. And guess what they have planned for you? Not much." [2]

– Jim Rohn, Business Philosopher (1930-2009)

"A goal without a plan is just a wish." [3]

– Antoine de Saint-Exupery, French writer (1900 - 1944)

"Deciding in advance when and where you will take specific actions to reach your goal can double or triple your chances for success." [4]

- Heidi Grant Halvorson, Columbia University Professor

The idea about planning your actions and achieving your goals isn't a random one. People who explicitly state when and where their new behaviors are going to happen are much more likely to stick to their goals.

Without a plan, it is like we are without our sight. We do not know where we are going and we do not have a structure to build upon. It is crucial to create a plan before we do anything else. When we start building in our mind how everything will play out, then the next steps and actions will appear in front of us without much effort. In the long run, we will end up saving a lot of time. Since we are doing all the thinking in advance, all we have to do is to follow the plan and make the necessary adjustments when needed.

When you are developing your plan, you need to know what you want to accomplish and establish a deadline (by when). Setting up measurable milestones is as important, since they will keep you in track with your goal and will give you a better understanding of your progress.

One of the biggest advantages of developing a plan is it will always be available to you, and you will not have to worry what action you need to take next. All you do is consistently follow your plan, not allowing reasons or excuses to divert you.

Your goal, and the type of actions you are going to take, should be tracked on a weekly plan, where activities are laid out on a daily basis. You need to take new actions every day; each action should have its own deadline. All these actions are part of the bigger plan to accomplish your goal. For example, the action of saving money and trying to close a deal with a larger client may be part of the bigger goal which may be to have enough money to take a trip to Europe.

At the end of your weekly plan, record results you produced and acknowledge yourself for your accomplishments. Then prepare the next week's weekly plan. Once again, instead of worrying all the time what needs to be done next, all you have to do is to follow the plan.

The very basic rule in the planning process is to "plan your work and work your plan". This means you need to carefully plan each step of the work you have to do, and then follow your plan religiously. Do not let anyone change your plan. Your plan should be in the centre and your whole life should orbit around your plan, and not the opposite.

How to Create an Effective Action Plan

Creating a powerful action plan always begins with having a clear purpose, a vision or goal in mind. Your action plan should be designed to take you from wherever you are at the moment directly to the accomplishment of your stated goal. With a well-designed plan and daily action, you can achieve virtually any goal you set out to accomplish. This is a step-by-step guide for creating an effective action plan:

1. Know where you are. Unless you know where you are, you are not going to be able to find the correct path to your destination.

2. Know where you're going. Every successful person knows the final goal and destination should be clear, otherwise you

wander for no reason. You need to know exactly what you want to accomplish and where you are going.

3. Be specific. Your goal should be **SMART** (**S**pecific, **M**easurable, **A**ttainable, **R**elevant, and **T**imely) and you need to create very specific tasks or steps that will move you toward the completion of that goal.

   With a goal and **SMART** objectives in place, the components of your action plan can be placed into a logical model that visually portrays your inputs, activities, outputs, and outcomes.

4. Create measurable milestones to help you evaluate your plan. Once you have a clear vision of the big picture, you need to set up the measurable milestones you need to hit throughout the time span of your project. These milestones will help you divide the work into smaller tangible goals and help you evaluate your plan and understand how far you have gone. Create milestones easily by starting at the end (the accomplishment of the goal) and work your way backwards to present day and circumstances.

   As you create measurable milestones, create also a list and accompanying timeline of specific action items or tasks to complete to hit those milestones.

5. Divide large tasks into smaller management projects. When we are dealing with large tasks we often feel intimidated and discouraged by the amount of work we have to do. When we break larger tasks down into smaller, more manageable chunks, it is easier to manage the work and we feel less stressed about executing our plan.

6. Put timelines on everything. No matter what action items you choose for which phase of your action plan; it is essential a timeframe be attached to absolutely everything.

    Without specific time frames and deadlines, you risk:

    a. Missing important deadlines that can set your entire project behind.

    b. Having some tasks never completed.

    c. Missing the opportunity to celebrate your accomplishments and strengthen your motivation for job well done.

7. Create a visual representation. Create a visual representation of your plan by using a flowchart, a Gantt chart, a spreadsheet, or some other type of business tool. The purpose of this is to make it easier to see where you are at a specific point in time and evaluate your progress quickly.

    a. Work your plan and don't stop until it's complete. Take daily action and follow up with anyone who may be helping you achieve your goal to ensure they are doing their part.

    b. Make adjustments as needed, but never give up on the goal. When, circumstances or unforeseen events prevent you from meeting deadlines, completing tasks, and achieving your goals don't be discouraged. Adjustments are absolutely necessary, especially when we have to adapt to change. When you miss a deadline, revise your plan and continue working to meet targets and to move forward.

Executing your plan

Take actions consistent with the plan you created. Be bold, audacious, and stand up for the opportunity to become who you want to be, and get what you want to have. Be a risk taker and live the possibility right now! Enrol and inspire others; share the possibility of your project/goal and who you are. Remember, the only thing stopping us in life is ourselves and the little voice telling us we cannot do this or that. We should not let our feelings and thoughts dishonor us. We should honor our word if we want to have a great life.

These are some helpful things to remember when you are executing your plan:

- Handle everything with a YES attitude. Be open to new opportunities that come your way and do not be afraid to say 'yes'. Don't let the fear of the unknown get the best of you and miss what might happen.

  Treat people with a YES attitude. When we are certain people will say NO to our ideas, then everything including our body language, voice, etc. appears like they will say no. If we act/believe they will say yes, then everything works in support. It all depends on how we interpret things. When we expect YES there is no fear of rejection. Create reasons that empower you and help you move forward rather than focusing on reasons things may go wrong.

- Remember, rejection is not a big deal. We often handle rejection as the worst thing that can happen to us. Because of this thinking, we hold back and do not take action. Regardless if rejection may, or may not happen, this will not eventually affect your life at the large scale you expect, since there are new opportunities everywhere. To deal with rejection, ask yourself "What is the absolutely worst thing that can happen?" Keep asking until you realize how you see rejection is a state of mind, and will not have a big effect on you.

- You can have everything in life you want – all at once. Often influenced by the limitations of others, we believe we have to make hard choices; we cannot have everything we want at the same time. Mostly, that is not true. Everything comes down to the way you manage your time, what is important to you, and your attitude towards things. When you have a "can do" attitude, everything is possible; you simply do not have to choose. It is possible to have everything you want and there are no limitations on what is possible.

- Act upon hunches. These are ideas that suddenly come into our mind at the most unexpected moments. When we have a shower, when we just wake up in the morning, while we are doing something else unrelated to our goal. Don't ignore these ideas. Write them down right away so you don't forget them, evaluate them and act upon them. Hunches come from our subconscious mind and intuition and may provide valuable guidance.

- Trust your instincts. In some cases, something may not feel right and you are getting a strange vibe, while in other cases, despite what everyone may tell you, you know you have to follow your instinct and move forward. You need to trust how you feel as usually you are right.

- Remember to have fun. While it is important to be committed to your goal, don't take everything too seriously; have fun, and laugh. Don't wait to reach your destination to enjoy; have fun on the way – celebrate your little victories.

- Be committed but not attached. While you should be committed to your goal and do everything in your power to make it happen, do not be attached to the final result. As long as you have done your very best, you will always know you tried and you can move with peace to other opportunities and new goals.

- Always be honest with yourself. If things do not go your way, you need to be honest with yourself and answer with integrity the following question "Have I done my absolute best to accomplish my goal, and did I take all the necessary actions and follow my instincts?" If the answer is no, then you know you need to refocus and continue your efforts.

- Don't be afraid to change the plan to meet your circumstances. You do not have to go to the gym to start exercising, just as you do not physically have to be in a building to take a university course. You can do it online. Think outside the box and what traditional performance is; discover new ways to do things to benefit you and help you accomplish what you want.

- Don't be afraid to set new rules, or change existing ones. We often talk about our modern way of life versus the life people used to live a couple of hundred years or more ago. The way of life and rules were different than what is now considered standard. This is an example illustrating eventually things change, and you should not be afraid to set new rules or change the ones that exist, when old ways of doing things don't work.

- Don't be afraid of change. Embrace change as it bring new opportunities and moves us forward. As President John F. Kennedy once said, "Change is the law of life. And those who look only to the past or present are certain to miss the future." [5] While you should be open to change, you need not try to change others and you should accept them for who they are.

- Move forward, no matter what. Stop thinking what other people are doing to you or all the obstacles before you; focus on how you are reacting to every situation. It is not what others do to you, but what you do to others.

- Open communication is essential for accomplishing any goal. Have open communication with everyone involved with your project and everyone who supports you to accomplish your goal.

- Remember it doesn't matter what you do, but how you do it. You accomplish goals by doing things in a certain way. Everything has to do with intent and the energy you are doing it with.

- Understand the importance of persistence. You may not get what you want right away. You persist; don't quit until your goal is accomplished.

- Announce to other people your goals and let them hold you accountable when you do not do what you said you will do. You may want to have a mentor and/or an accountability partner who will be there to support and motivate you the whole way.

- Reach out and ask for help. Don't let your ego get the best of you. People are eager to help you accomplish your goals with time, money, or anything else you want, as long as you touch, move, and inspire them. See others as possibilities, and ask for help. Opportunities to get help to accomplish your goals are everywhere.

- Be a true leader. Believe in yourself, and also believe in others. A true leader creates opportunities for him/herself, helps others realize their own dreams, and creates a future for the community he/she is living in. Be generous, trust and motivate others to reach their goals, give them the opportunity to show their skills by leading; help them accomplish whatever is important to them. By creating leaders, you produce expanded results, and by creating large opportunities for others, you are coming closer to becoming an authority figure in your industry, if that is what you want.

- Aim to become an authority figure in your field, a thought leader, who sets the tone for his/her industry and people accept it. Your main responsibility is to continue growing, innovating, and sharing your knowledge.

176

- Reward yourself; celebrate small wins. At the start of a big project, break it up into smaller chunks, each with its own goal and reward. You'll have something to look forward to when each stage is completed.

Tools that can help us to follow through with our plan

Use tools that can help and support you follow through with your plan. These are some recommendations:

- Put your plan into an existing system like a calendar. One or two planned actions will change your life and produce results.

- Send yourself reminders for actions you need to take.

- Take notes and write down your ideas as they come.

- Use mind maps.

- Ask others to hold you accountable.

- Find a working buddy or people who have the same goals.

- Talk to mentors – people who have been there and done that and are willing to share their knowledge.

Use If-Then Planning To Achieve Any Goal

While we want to be focused with laser-like precision to get things done, we are often distracted, procrastinate, or end up doing things that are less important and not at the top of our priorities.

Luckily, enough there is a strategy that helps us deal effectively with distractions. This strategy is called if-then; it is a powerful way to help you achieve any goal.

The if-then strategy is based on the idea that if we decide in advance when and where we will take specific actions to accomplish our goals, we can double or triple the chances of success. This strategy has the following format:

If X happens, then I will do Y.

This strategy is very effective, because it enables us to seize the critical moment, even if we are busy doing other things and because we humans are particularly good at encoding and remembering information in "If X, then Y" terms and ultimately guide our behavior by those terms.

These are two examples of the If-then planning:

- If I am getting too distracted by colleagues, then I will stick to a 5 minute chat limit and head back to work.

- If it is 3pm, then I will spend 30 minutes to read and respond to important emails.

This strategy can been successful for any goal you can think of, personal or professional, and of any size.

CHAPTER 17

THE POWER OF ALL

"It is literally true that you can succeed best and quickest by helping others to succeed." [1]

– Napoleon Hill, Personal Success Author

When people work together and support each other towards a common goal, they create a collective power that has more strength than any individual effort. As long as everyone involved in this effort is aligned towards that same goal, there is a huge probability the results will be multiplied and achieved in less time. This collective effort has the potential to benefit in unpredictable ways everyone involved, but above all it will benefit the one(s) who initiated the effort. This can happen by helping the initiators stay focused and on track, by giving them access to new knowledge and resources, as well as emotional support and encouragement in times of doubt. Friends, colleagues, family – even strangers – are potential members of this collective force that helps you achieve your goals.

Looking back, I'm often amazed that once I used to believe I can do everything on my own. I was so confident, almost foolish I would say, I used to think I did not need anybody and I could accomplish everything I wanted by counting only on my own powers. I did not realize I was putting limitations on myself and the possibility to get things done, getting a fresh point of view, and accomplishing the goals I was going after, much faster.

Asking help from others, to accomplish your personal or professional goals, is one of the wisest things you can do. This help may take different forms and shapes. It may take the form of emotional support and encouragement, it can be financial help, or it can be what is described in the business world by the word 'delegation'. Delegation is the assignment of responsibility or authority to another person to carry out specific activities; yet while they have the opportunity, many leaders do not delegate and prefer to do things on their own.

There is no reason to burn yourself out and be alone in your effort. People are willing to offer a helping hand, to be there to support you, if you ask them. All you need to do is ask. Once you have a goal, start planning how you will accomplish your goal, while placing everyone who you think can help you, in your plan. You need to think who you should include in your plan and why, the type and size of help you need (example: time, money, etc.), how they can help you, and why they should help you (what is it in for them?). People can potentially become a big part of your plan and support you, as long as you allow them to participate. All you need to do is ask. If you do not ask, you will not get. If you receive a negative answer, you should not see it as a defeat, or take it personally.

How you should approach others to help you

When you approach others to ask for help, be honest, open, and direct. You should have integrity, be yourself, and be willing to openly share your true passions, goals, experiences, fears, and dreams. Don't be afraid to touch, move, and inspire others with your passions. You should actually seek to do that. Almost as important, before you even approach someone, be clear about what you want, and what others should expect by helping you.

You may want to prepare a different pitch/approach depending on who you are talking to. This is very important especially if you are planning to approach larger groups and different communities. You should remember the connection between you and them happens on the mental level. It is about how you use words and create images, and how those images are projected and perceived in the minds of the people you are talking to. Of course the mental drives the emotional and you want to persuade at the emotional level too.

The fear of rejection and simply being too proud, may often prevent us from asking for help – you should be eager to take risks, put yourself out there, trust others, and genuinely believe things will go your way. While you ask for their help, you need to have great listening skills and seek for gold. Their answer might be "no", but they may offer ideas or another way to help you, or give you genuine advice. If someone is not able to help you, they may know someone who will. When you share yourself with others, always remember you may find supporters where you least expect. All you have to do is take the risk.

Always show gratitude; appreciate the time it took for someone to listen to you, and be willing to return the favor. Maybe you offer your genuine advice for an issue important to them, or provide help for something that can benefit them. If you do not receive someone's support, this should not stop you from offering yours. At the end, it is not about what others do – that is something we cannot control. It is about what we do and how we can be there for others. We should always lead by example and always take a stand for ourselves and others.

Be generous and be willing to help others accomplish their goals. By helping, you may create the opportunity for others to mentor you. At the end, a good deed in nature will always come back to you in another way.

The roles of other people in helping you

The right people are always willing to help you depending on your goals, what you really need, what you are willing to offer (example: opportunity to others to express themselves/manage a project), and how valuable they see what they are going to get back in return (example: the opportunity to work with you towards a common goal, or be part of a community).

Any type of help is important as long as we are able to recognize its value and appreciate it. Others may help you by providing their time or money, by offering a listening ear and honest feedback, by mentoring you, holding you accountable, motivating you, or just being there and supporting you emotionally. While some may not be able to help you directly, they may provide valuable advice and direct you to the people you need to meet or guide you to the right resources.

Building a strong support system – a team of people who are aligned with your goals and who help you get there is definitely a huge advantage you should not overlook. Build a team with people you can trust, whose knowledge and judgment you respect, who have common sense, and a bright mind and desire to support you to reach your goals.

Why others will help you

There are many reasons why people may want to help you thrive and succeed which you may have not considered. Here are a few of these reasons:

- They simply like you, and the way you may make them feel. There may not be any other specific reason.

- For some people, it is their nature and they genuinely find happiness and enjoyment helping others. It gives them purpose.

- They are inspired by you and what you do; they believe in you and they want genuinely to help you achieve your goals.

- They see you as someone who listens, enrolls others, sees potential in others, and creates opportunities for him/herself and others. Simply, they see you as a leader and they want to support you. Through you, they may see the opportunity to accomplish their own goals and dreams, to learn and to expand their horizons.

- People who've known us for years, friends and family, want to take a leap to help us succeed, but they don't know how. Sharing our goals and asking their help, we give them the opportunity to contribute towards our growth.

- They may want to help as a return of a favor, or show their appreciation for something you did for them long time ago.

- Successful people genuinely like sharing their knowledge and skills and helping others succeed.

- A few of the basic human needs are the need of belonging, companionship, and the feeling they are needed. By helping you, others have the opportunity to fulfil those needs.

- We are all in this together – helping others is like helping ourselves. In this win-win formula, we may gain new knowledge and new experiences that we haven't counted on.

Once you ask people to help you, and they accept your invitation, then hold them accountable for the promise they made. Ask them to take actions right away and hold them accountable if they do not fulfil what you asked for.

People are willing to help you

Next time you have a personal or professional goal, share it with a friend, colleague, or someone who is considered an expert in their field; ask them to support you or mentor you. You will be amazed how many people will be eager to support your cause and be there for you.

CHAPTER 18

SEEKING EXCELLENCE

*"We are what we repeatedly do. Excellence, then, is not an act,
but a habit."* [1]

– Aristotle, Greek Philosopher

I n a world full of mediocrity, seeking excellence at every
level of your life is what will truly differentiate you and will
give you the extra edge you need to accomplish everything
you desire. As Aristotle said, "we are what we repeatedly do".
As seeking excellence becomes a habit, you constantly motivate
yourself to go above and beyond to reach your goals. Seeking
excellence becomes the fuel in accomplishing goals often
considered unthinkable to reach.

What is excellence?

There are many definitions of excellence, and we all have our
own interpretation as to what we consider excellence. We often
use excellence as a term to describe superiority, and we end up
comparing people, accomplishments, and situations as being
excellent or not. The term can often become very vague, and we
do not have clarity as to what it really means. Not understanding
what excellence means often scares us, intimidates us and we end

up stopping to seek for it. Excellence may seem too difficult to accomplish, it may seem it will take too much time and effort, and often we see it as something happening in the distant future. We often associate excellence with awards and we feel recognition by others will be the true indication we excel. As we all have our own story about excellence, we need to deal with the facts and see what is possible.

We start with the assumption excellence is a possibility we want to achieve. Excellence, as a possibility, does not belong in the future or the past. Excellence belongs in the present moment and is happening every second we live and we are aware of our environment and who we are. Excellence is happening now, and now, and now and is the stand we take and are, allowing us to perform at levels previously not possible, thus creating new ground to discover. Excellence is being in life, right now, intending for the fulfillment of a new possibility. We excel when we are focused and we do the best we can, at the specific moment, under any circumstances. We excel when at the present moment, we are not afraid to reach our limits and explore new territories. What happened yesterday belongs to the past and what will happen in the future is unknown and not certain. We need to excel now, and be committed to perform at our full capabilities at this very present moment.

Excellence is generated moment moment-by-moment. There is no comparison, worse or better, and there is no past to overcome or future to get to. As you pursue your goals, simply seek excellence at all times.

How do we achieve excellence?

Every present moment is the opportunity for creating and reaching excellence. While you should not worry about the past or the future, you need to make up your mind you will be in the success zone – what I call the 'mindful excellence zone' – at each present moment.

Each present moment is an opportunity to take action and perform the best you can at every level of your life. If you are a professional, become the best at what you do, offer the best products and services possible, and go above and beyond for your clients. In your family life, be the best father or mother, sister or brother, son or daughter you can be. If you are exercising and you feel extremely tired, don't give up, keep on moving forward and do the best you can at that present moment. There are countless opportunities every day to achieve excellence. The top three ingredients of reaching excellence should be:

a.   Focus on the present moment.

b.   Take action.

c.   Do the best you can.

In your effort to do things to the best of your abilities, try to better understand what you do, how you do it, and why you do it. Studying, practising, and having laser-like focus will help you a great deal. Question yourself – why you do what you do and how can you improve – and read books to expand your knowledge, understanding of things, and increase the level of your awareness. In addition, change your complaints into opportunities, and use practical tools and techniques to increase performance. Some of these tools and techniques are mentioned throughout this book (example: Pomodoro Technique).

No one stays where they are and results may get better or worse. Don't get disempowered if at times you do not perform at the best of your abilities. Give yourself room to take a break; acknowledge and celebrate your accomplishments and all your hard work up to that point. Then restart fresh, applying again the same principles – focusing on the present moment, taking action, and doing the best you can. In the process, remember to respect and honour yourself and others and while you may accept or request help, you should always have confidence in yourself and your capabilities.

"You can start right where you stand and apply the habit of going the extra mile by rendering more service and better service than you are now being paid for." [2]

– Napoleon Hill, Personal Success Author

"It has always been my belief that a man should do his best, regardless of how much he receives for his services, or the number of people he may be serving, or the class of people he served. If you are to clean toilets then you should aim to be the best toilet cleaner out there." [3]

– Napoleon Hill, Personal Success Author

CHAPTER 19

EVALUATE YOUR PLAN

"When defeat comes, accept it as a signal that your plans are not sound, rebuild those plans, and set sail once more toward your coveted goal." [1]

– Napoleon Hill, Personal Success Author

Evaluation is a process that critically assesses a plan. It involves collecting and analyzing information about the activities, characteristics, and outcomes of a plan to make judgments about the plan, improve plan effectiveness, and/or inform decisions about future plan development. [2] Evaluation offers a way to determine whether an initiative has been worthwhile in terms of delivering what was intended and expected. However, good evaluation can also answer other important questions.

Evaluation should be part of your overall plan and you should not leave it for the end. The evaluation experience is likely to be more positive and its results are likely to be more useful, if you build evaluation in from the start, and make it an on-going activity. Evaluate your plan at selected milestones you have set up to track the progress of your plan, but also evaluate your plan when you see that things are not going the way you want. This is the time you need to reassess.

There are eight steps to developing an evaluation plan

1. Develop evaluation questions (What do you want to know?)

2. Determine indicators (What will you measure? What type of data will you need to answer the evaluation questions?)

3. Identify data sources (Where can you find these data?)

4. Determine the data collection method (How will you gather the data?)

5. Specify the time frame for data collection (When will you collect the data?)

6. Plan the data analysis (How will data be analyzed and interpreted?)

7. Communicate results (With whom and how will results be shared?)

8. Designate responsibility (Who will oversee completion of this evaluation?)

Evaluation though doesn't have to be as complicated, especially when it comes to goals that are personal; not business-related, or only involve you. Take this time to assess the goal process – from inception to completion. If you feel it took too long to achieve this goal, examine your stumbling blocks. Start by asking questions that will help you understand the current situation and help you plan the next steps. Questions may include:

- What are the resources I have put towards accomplishing my goal? This may include time, effort, personal sacrifices, etc.?

- Have I accomplished my goals up to this moment?

- Are the goals I set up reasonable or possible?

- What changes can I make to ensure my plans are feasible/workable?

- Are there any skills I need to acquire before trying to complete other goals?

- If I learned something about the way I work towards meeting my goal, is it something that can be applied to other goals?

While there are many questions you can ask to evaluate your plan, you can cut short the process by asking these top 3 questions which will give you all the crucial information you need and can potentially change your life:

a. What am I doing?

b. What works?

c. What doesn't work?

Then all you have to do is stop doing what doesn't work, and put all your energy and time into what does work.

Things you need to take into consideration when you evaluate your plan. These may apply depending on the goals you want to accomplish.

- **Keep track of your progress.** Keeping a record – journal or computer – is a great way to keep track of both personal and professional progress. Checking in with yourself, and acknowledging the progress made towards a certain goal is key to staying motivated.

- **Be adaptable and open to change.** When things do not work, due to external indicators or because there is something you do not do right, do not be afraid to make all the changes needed for the plan to work. Many people fail because they are not open to change. I see change as a necessary step to moving forward. Adjust your plan based on the new facts and information and go ahead with the new plans.

- **Find an observer.** An observer is someone who is not directly involved with your plan (friend, mentor, relative, etc.) and is not affected by the outcome of your plan, with whom you can talk about your plan and who can give you an honest opinion and advice. Sometimes people who are not directly involved, or have nothing at stake, may see obvious things that are in front of us but we do not see and who can offer a valuable point of view.

- Asking a friend with similar goals to **collaborate with you** is a great way to keep you motivated and to make sure you hit your goal target dates.

- **Find a leader.** While you are working on your plan you may realize what you do is not enough. Maybe it is time you have to find a leader. This is someone who can take your project to the next level or can simply mentor you and help you go where you need to be.

- **Acknowledge yourself.** Take time to reflect and acknowledge yourself often for all the wonderful things you have accomplished. That is one of the major mistakes we often make. We are so focused on the big goal, we do not acknowledge all the small victories and things accomplished.

- **Celebrate your victories (or reward your accomplishments).** Go with the people who matter to you, and celebrate your victories. You may choose to buy something for yourself as a reward or do something different to celebrate your accomplishments. Whatever you do, take time to celebrate key milestones to refuel your engine and to give you strength to move forward.

- **Have integrity with yourself.** Be honest with yourself; don't allow reasons or excuses to get in the way. Have you done everything you said you will do to accomplish your goal? Have you done what others expect from you? Sometimes we lie to ourselves knowing we can become our biggest critic. This doesn't help us. If things do not go the way we want, we have to find out what really happened. Most of the time, WE hold ourselves back, not others.

- **Results are results.** Accept the fact results are results, regardless if they are positive or negative. Sometimes even negative results may produce a chain reaction that will eventually produce positive results. Of course, you would prefer positive results, but that is not always possible. You have to acknowledge yourself for taking action. Sometimes it is all that matters to eventually produce positive results.

- **Be committed but not attached.** While you need to be committed to accomplish your goals, and do the best you can in your power, you should not be attached with the final outcome. Not accomplishing a goal will not be the end of your life and there will always be other opportunities to give you the same sense of excitement and feeling of accomplishment.

- **Don't quit (unless your goal does not inspire you any more).** Patience, persistence, and hard work make an unbeatable combination for success. Success though doesn't always come exactly when we want it, and we may face temporary defeat and perhaps failure. And sometimes, when we are so close to enjoying the fruits of our efforts, we lose faith and we just give up. If you are really passionate about your goal and you want something badly, do not give up until you make it happen. Let it consume you; let it become your main purpose. However, if during your evaluation you realize your goal does not inspire you any more, do not be afraid to change direction and explore other goals and opportunities that motivate you and inspire you.

- Remember you need **to let go of the attachment of producing results or changing others.** Just let go; focus on your goals, and not the results.

What happens when plans fall apart?

These are some quick strategies you can try when plans seem to fall apart:

1) **Apply an "if __ then__" strategy.**

The "if–then" strategy gives you a clear plan for overcoming the unexpected stuff, which means it's less likely the urgencies of life will have a huge impact on you. You do not have control as to when little emergencies may happen to you, but when and if they happen, you can be as prepared as possible.

This is an example of an "if _ then_" strategy: If I eat ice-cream while I diet, then I will not eat ice-cream for a week.

2) **Review, Re-evaluate, and Revise.**

If things do not work out the way you hoped, find out what happened, learn how to avoid the same mistakes in the future, and try again. Failures are just lessons pointing you toward success.

The first step is to review the steps you took and the process you followed. Re-evaluate by examining what went wrong and where. What didn't work? What could you have done better? Did you have all the necessary skills and tools? Your findings will be most revealing, and in turn, allow you to set up a better, more comprehensive approach. The second step is to revise and improve the current strategy. The third and last step is to apply the new strategy. Keep in mind developing a successful plan is not a cookie-cutter process and you may have to adjust your plans many times.

3) **Change Your Strategy.**

Insanity is to keep doing the same thing again and again, and expecting different results. [3] If you have been applying for a long time your original strategy, but you find you're continually hitting road bumps, you may need to tweak your approach. It is very possible you are not doing the right things and you need to change your strategy and try again.

"When something goes wrong in your life, just yell "Plot twist!" and move on."

– unknown

4) **Repeat your Efforts.**

You might be doing all the right things, but it is possible the timing is not right. Repeating the same exact actions enough times will bring success. Character is built during the third and fourth attempts at achieving a goal, not the first try.

CHAPTER 20

HOW TO GET AND STAY MOTIVATED

M otivation is the force that guides our behaviors, the reason causing us to take action. Whether a person succeeds, fails, or leads, depends on his or her ability to keep motivated. Getting to know the intricacies of your own motivation can have lasting effects. Understanding and acting upon the things that motivate you, you begin to understand what it means to live a healthy, happy life.

The question is, 'what motivates you?' If you work for someone else, is it the pressure from your boss or the love for your job? If you're in business for yourself, is it the pressure from a customer or your thirst for success? If you want to start exercising, is it because you want to look good for yourself, for others, or you want to have a healthy and strong body? Whatever the answer, it's important to recognize we are all motivated by something. If we weren't, nothing would ever get accomplished.

But how, you ask? How do you motivate yourself, and stay motivated long enough to achieve success? These are some of the things that affect motivation:

1. **Identify Your Purpose:** Your ultimate goal and purpose may be the only thing you need to motivate you to accomplish anything you desire.

How do you find your purpose though? You need to answer these simple questions honestly:

a.   Who are you? Dig deep in your soul; find the true YOU no one may know.

b.   What do you **really** want from life?

c.   Do you have the desire to impact the life of other people?

d.   What is it you have others will benefit from receiving?

e.   What are the things that make you really happy and you can't live without?

When you answer these questions, you will get a better understanding as to what your purpose is. You need to accept and evaluate the answers as they are. You may not like some of the answers because they may not agree with the normal social standards or your current situation, and your current beliefs. At the end you have to be true to yourself. If you want to be happy, you need to go after what you really want and not what others expect from you.

2.   **Find the good reasons:** Have you ever asked yourself what are the real reasons you are doing something? Often we do things as a result of habit. We have been doing the same thing over and over again without knowing why we are doing it – this is what we have been used to doing. On the other hand, we do so many things on a daily basis because we have strong reasons to do them. We follow a healthy diet because we want to stay healthy. We may exercise because we

want to look great, and we may work hard because we want to be able to buy the best things life has to offer. Those good reasons – a material reward, a personal gain, or a feeling of accomplishment are what motivates us and brings us closer to our bigger goal. Write down those reasons with a pen. Studies show when we write by hand and connect the letters manually, we engage the brain more actively in the process. Because typing is an automatic function that involves merely selecting letters, there's less of a mental connection. When criticism from others or self-doubt makes you question if you can accomplish those goals, go back and read those good reasons. They will motivate you and help you carry on.

3. **Act with the higher purpose in mind:** Activities and actions that do not serve your higher purpose, should be minimized and even completely avoided. Watching countless hours of TV will not serve your purpose unless you want to become a TV critic. If that is your purpose, go ahead by all means – if it is not your purpose, you are wasting your time when you can do so many other things that serve your goals.

4. **Make each day count:** As we don't have all the time in the world, focus on today and do the things you really want to do.

5. **Treat inaction as the only real failure:** Without taking action, nothing is accomplished. Action is the beginning and the end of everything. If you don't take action, you fail by default and can't learn from experiences. When you take action, you motivate yourself by exploring and discovering new possibilities, and this keeps you going.

6. **Forgive your mistakes:** When you know you have made a mistake, you have to acknowledge it. You should not be harsh; forgive yourself for having made a mistake and then let it go. "Forgiving yourself for your mistakes increases motivation and engagement with goals," Kelly McGonigal, a Stanford psychologist and author of The Willpower Instinct (Avery, 2011), says, "When you forgive your mistakes, you create the room to bounce back and grow at the same time." [1]

7. **Be happy:** A great deal of motivation comes from understanding one's state of happiness. While happiness is an objective concept – the things that make us happy may be different from one person to another – there are some things we can do to increase our happiness and eventually our motivation. Please revisit Chapter 12 and read some of the things you can do to increase your happiness.

8. **Keep your energy levels high:** There is a direct connection between our motivation and the levels of our own energy. As long as our energy is high, then our motivation is high as well. When our energy is low, especially after a long day at work or when we pull that all-nighter, then our motivation decreases drastically. Keeping your energy levels high is crucial.

These are some factors that affect your level of energy:

What you eat: When your body needs energy, seek it out, because it will be extremely hard to stay **motivated** without it. Here are twelve power foods that'll give a powerful boost to your daily diet [2]:

a. **Carbohydrates:** Carbohydrates offer fuel to the body in the form of glucose, which is the best energy source for the brain and central nervous system – two vital body systems.

b. **Brown Rice:** Rich in manganese, the mineral that helps produce energy from protein and carbs, it will help you maintain high energy all day.

c. **Sweet Potato:** High in carbohydrates and loaded with beta-carotene (vitamin A) and vitamin C, these will help fight off midday fatigue.

d. **Honey:** Low on the glycemic index, this natural sweetener is a time-released muscle fuel during exercise, replenishing muscles post-workout.

e. **Fruits:** Fruit offers a significant dose of glucose, which your body can easily metabolize into energy. Most fruits can be digested in under half an hour, which makes them a quick, nutritious way to get a burst of energy.

f. **Bananas:** Because they are composed mostly of sugars (glucose, fructose, and sucrose) and fiber, bananas are a foolproof energy food.

g. **Apples:** High in fiber, apples take longer to digest, so they'll give you a more prolonged powerful jolt of energy than many other fruit picks.

h. **Oranges:** High in vitamin C, potassium and folate, this citrus fruit rations out energy steadily over time instead of giving you a quick sugar rush.

i. **Food derived from plants:** Foods that come straight from a tree or plant will help you maintain energy levels. Certain veggies have all the proteins, carbs, and good fats you need to keep you going all day. Plus, some nuts, such as almonds will help to regulate your protein intake.

j. **Spinach:** Spinach is an excellent source of iron, a key component of energy production in the body.

k. **Beans:** Both a protein and a complex carb, they're a must for both carnivores and vegetarians.

l. **Almonds:** Packed with protein, manganese, copper and riboflavin, almonds are a handy snack to keep at your desk or in your bag.

High proteins: Protein is an essential energy food – particularly when you're trying to drop a few pounds. If you are, replace part of your regular carbohydrate intake with proteins; this will help ensure your muscle mass remains constant as your body metabolizes fat cells as a source of energy.

a. **Salmon:** Salmon contains protein and vitamin B6, niacin and riboflavin – all of which help convert the food you eat into energy.

b. **Yogurt:** Rich in magnesium, which is crucial for the release of energy, yogurt also adds a dose of calcium to your diet. Enjoy it post-workout to help replenish your glycogen sources.

c. **Eggs:** Containing the highest complete form of protein in any food, (a whopping 97% of it can be absorbed by your body!), eggs provide 30% of your daily value of protein. All of the essential amino acids your body uses to rebuild muscle can also be found in eggs.

Water: Water makes up the major fluid supporting our bodily systems and is an important source of energy. The Institute of Medicines reports men need about 3 liters of water while women require about 2.2 liters but these numbers include total beverages in a day plus water-rich foods [3]. When you have a headache, before you grab those pills in your medicine cabinet, try putting some water into your system. Drink a glass or two, wait for fifteen minutes, and see if the headache is gone [4].

Replace short-lived energy sources: Short-lived energy sources such as coffee and energy drinks, can give you a quick boost but will wear off shortly after consumption and cause you to crash. Consider replacing those sources with vitamins, especially the family of B vitamins.

a. The family of B vitamins, which are also known as B complex vitamins, play an important role in converting food into energy and helping the body metabolize fats and proteins. Two important vitamins of this group of 8 vitamins are B6 and B12 [5].

b. "Vitamin B6 helps many systems in your body function," says Dee Sandquist, MS, RD, CD, spokesperson for the American Dietetic Association. "It is important for cardiovascular, digestive, immune, muscular, and nervous system function. It is one of the vitamins behind the scenes." Excellent sources of vitamin B6 include beef, poultry, fish, and eggs [6].

c.   Vitamin B12 helps form DNA, make healthy blood cells, and keep nerves working properly. The best sources of Vitamin B12 include: eggs, milk, cheese, milk products, meat (especially liver), fish, and seafood (especially clams, oysters and mussels), and poultry.

Sleep: Sleep is nature's downtime. Make sure you get enough of it – about nine hours every night. The quality of your sleep is as important as the hours you sleep. These are some tips to help you improve the quality of your sleep:

a.   Stick to a sleep schedule, even on weekends, holidays, and days off.

b.   Pay attention to what you eat and drink before sleep; avoid nicotine, caffeine and alcohol.

c.   Create a bedtime ritual to tell your body it's time to wind down [7]. This might be a warm bath or shower, reading a book, or listening to soothing music.

d.   Get comfortable and create a room good for sleeping: Make sure your bedroom is completely dark and cool at night, ideally 65 degrees (18 Celsius), and there are no sounds keeping you awake. Your mattress and pillow can contribute to better sleep, too. Since features of good bedding are subjective, choose what feels most comfortable to you.

9. **Use language that inspires you:** The language we use to describe what we want stealthily affects outcomes. Avoid words and expressions that hold you back such as, "I'll try…","One day I might…", "who knows, maybe…" and replace them with goals that will define your success, "I will", "I can", "I have no doubt I will achieve this…", etc. In the same context, think before you speak and avoid expressing thoughts that do not serve your purpose.

10. **Be efficient:** Efficiency is the ability to accomplish something with the least waste of time and effort. Efficiency is extremely important since without it a person has limited motivation to do anything. Efficiency can be developed. These are some of the things you can do to develop efficiency:

    a. Develop your skills: If you have a skill you are good at it, don't be afraid to use it. In addition, if you have a skill you want to be better at, don't procrastinate – practice. Find the time to train and discover new skills. Remember practice makes perfect!

    b. Don't afraid to compete: Efficiency is drawn from reference, and competition gives us the opportunity to create a reference point. When we compete, we are able to understand our own self value and this helps and drive us to become better at what we do. In turn, this enhances our effectiveness or capability to produce results.

11. **Get the support you need:** By seeking and finding the right support, we have greater chances of increasing our motivation and accomplishing our goals. Support can be broken down into two areas, internal and external:

a. Internal Support: this is the support we provide ourselves, and includes all the good reasons we give ourselves something is worth doing. Those reasons are not necessarily true, and are good only if they inspire us to move in the right direction and to our goal.

Our motivation often comes from our internal drive to succeed, our ability to make decisions and stick with them, and the ability to turn our flaws into something positive and productive. Examples are: turning procrastination to action, turning impatience to patience, and aggression to ambition.

b. External Support: this is the support we get from people including family and friends, places (example a beautiful landscape), or things that motivate us and inspire us to reach our full potential. A strong support system can really make a difference between having the motivation to achieve our goals or not. On the other hand, a weak support system has the potential to discourage and stop us from going after what we want. While external support can have a huge influence on us, we need to use common sense and good judgment, reject negative influences, and get strength from those who are there to support each of our steps. As it is not always easy to reach our objectives on our own, don't be shy to ask for support. Not only will you get help and a different point of view, but also by announcing your intentions, you send a strong message to the world and, more important, to your unconscious mind, which can sometimes sabotage your best efforts.

12. **Avoid negative people and reprogram your information intake:** Negative people waste your time, drain your energy, and challenge your motivation for no reason. From their own point of view, they may not see things happening, or they may not want you to succeed. As important as it is to focus on your goal, it is equally important to avoid negative people at all costs.

    Negative people though are not always what can hold us back. Negative and cynical thoughts from the media and society may have the same impact. Reduce your information intake. Then program in positive news and entertainment, more of your own thoughts, and useful information such as personal growth tapes and books. Be selective and keep it positive [8].

13. **Fulfilment:** Fulfilment is a strong element that can drastically boost your motivation. Take the time to step back and appreciate what you have already accomplished. Don't be afraid to take credit for what you have done – accept gracefully praise and admiration from others and use all the positive thoughts and energy as a fuel to move forward.

14. **Reach your goals every day:** When we set, and accomplish every day small goals, we build momentum and empowerment. Those goals may be as simple as following through and calling a friend, reading a chapter of a book on your way to work, or exercise for 10 minutes. The accomplishment of small goals is considered victory and this keeps our motivation high to accomplish other bigger goals. In addition, it has been scientifically proven that writing down goals makes us more

successful. Prepare a new checklist every day and cross off goals as they are done.

15. **One Goal:** When you try to take on too much and accomplish many goals at once, you cannot maintain energy and focus and you end up challenging your motivation. You have to prioritize, choose, and focus on one goal at a time. You can always go after your other goals when you have accomplished the one that is at the top of your list.

16. **Monitor your goals:** To motivate yourself on a daily basis, you must set goals and monitor them on a daily basis. A good tool for doing that is by applying the "Eisenhower Method". Read about this method in Chapter 23.

17. **Recognize your progress:** It is human nature to want things to happen at once. Even when we split goals into smaller tasks and milestones, we often are not satisfied until the goal is fully completed. When we recognize our progress, we take the time to look at the bigger picture and realize where exactly we are, and how much more we have left to do. When we recognize the positive difference and progress made, we get empowered and we find the motivation to continue [9].

18. **Visualize your goal:** We think in images; when we visualize a goal, our subconscious mind doesn't know if it is real or not, good or bad. When we visualize accomplishing our goal, we put it into the sphere of reality and this motivates us to go after it no matter what. Spend 10-15 minutes a day and visualize yourself accomplishing your goal. See it. Feel it. Believe it. To give you a different perspective, elite athletes

visualize their performance ahead of time – right down to the last second they cross the finish line.

You may also want to write down your goals and the reasons for working towards them and place them somewhere visible. This may be by your computer or the bathroom mirror. This will remind you of your goals throughout the day and it will be easier to stay on track and focused.

19. **Break the goal down into smaller pieces:** Neuroscience tells us each small success triggers the brain's reward center, releasing feel-good chemical neurotransmitters. These help focus our concentration, and motivate us to take another similar step. To achieve often small successes, you need to break down the goal into smaller pieces. If you do not, you will quickly get overwhelmed and unable to handle stress you face to accomplish your big goal. This is also a good way to prevent yourself from wanting to give up [10].

20. **Build on small successes and create flow:** If you find it difficult to find motivation, start building your excitement and motivation by setting and accomplishing goals that at the beginning are very easy. Just clean your desk. Or pay your bills. This will help you build the muscle to eventually achieve much bigger goals. If your goal is to lose weight, instead of setting up a goal that is scary and difficult to accomplish (example to lose 10 pounds within a week), set a goal to lose 1 pound within a two week period. Starting at a slow pace, will help you get started and prepare you for the next bigger thing. When you find a task difficult, always remember to take baby steps, and set yourself up for success by building on small victories [11].

21. **Remember your successes:** Use a journal and write down your successes to remind yourself what you can accomplish if you put your mind to it.

22. **Get excited:** When we are excited about a goal, we have the energy to move forward and keep going. But, how do we get excited when we do not feel motivated? One good way to build our excitement is by faking it. The strange thing is, within a few minutes you actually start to feel motivated or enthusiastic for real. Write down your goal and the benefits for accomplishing your goal; read it many times every day in front of a mirror. Then memorize it and be as excited as possible, and believe you have already accomplished your goal. How would it feel if you actually have what you already want? Grab that feeling and let it guide you and increase your excitement.

    Visualizing accomplishing your goal, reading anything related to your goal, sharing your goal with others, and building on their excitement and happiness for you, are all good ways to get excited and keep the momentum.

23. **Have a strategy, but be prepared to change course:** If a certain approach doesn't work for you, find another one, and keep trying until you find the one which will keep you motivated and get you the desired results. No plan should be cast in concrete, and it should not be more important than achieving the goal. Thomas Edison once said, "I have not failed. I've just found 10,000 ways that won't work." It is common for humans to try to find an easy way out by admitting defeat and giving up, rather than trying to find a different solution to their problem. If you really want to

accomplish your goal, there is always a way – all you have to do is find a different approach. Keep on trying and do not give up, no matter what [12].

24. **See the big picture:** The way you see the world and your position in it, can be a great source of motivation and a reason to turn your motivation into action. Why are you here? What is your ultimate purpose in life? How do you see yourself in the big scheme of things? You may want to try to find answer to those questions.

25. **Take responsibility for your own results:** A lot of people use excuses, blame others for their own mishaps, and believe luck and fate is the reason they are not accomplishing results. They do not understand they are the commanders of their own life and fate, and nothing can get in their way unless they decide to let it get in their way. Taking responsibility for our own results is the first step to acknowledging we have absolute control of our lives and it is up to us to achieve whatever we desire.

26. **Frequently read books, quotes, and success stories from thought leaders who can motivate you:** The true difference between success and failure is your ability to get and keep yourself motivated. Find inspiration from others who have already achieved what you want to achieve. Read books, magazines, quotes, and success stories, or listen to motivational/personal audio while you are on the move (driving, riding the bus or bike, etc.) The positive energy of others, and their new ideas, will rub off on you and you can imitate their success strategies. Remember, people who motivate you are people just like you. So let them inspire

you, instead of just looking up at them admiringly. Here are 10 thoughts motivational guru Omar Periu shared with Geoffrey James, a contributing editor for Inc.com that I find very inspiring [13]:

a. Motivation means choosing to do what you'd rather not do, which is why unmotivated people never get anywhere.

b. Most people want to improve their situation, but few take responsibility for motivating themselves to make changes.

c. People can always validate the decision to avoid unpleasant work. Example: "Today, I'll get organized; tomorrow I'll make cold calls."

d. Motivation comes from managing your mind and your emotions. Fail at this and you'll live a life of quiet desperation.

e. The most depressing and de-motivating sentences in the world usually begin with the phrase "Someday, I'll..."

f. If you find yourself thinking negative thoughts, go someplace quiet and replace those thoughts with positive affirmations, prayer, or meditation.

g. To get big results, ask yourself big questions. "Why do I want to be a millionaire?" is far more motivating than "How can I make a living?"

h. Don't set goals that just excite you; set goals that scare you a little bit. That way they'll strengthen your "motivation muscle."

i. What holds people back is fear of failure, but if you don't take action, you'll fail by default, so what have you got to lose?

j. You can have whatever you want in life, but nobody is going to give it to you. Everything of value must be earned.

27. **Build anticipation:** When we have a new goal, we often want to get into it right away. While it is important to take action and commit right away, when you build anticipation, you increase your focus and energy towards your goal. An example is taking a trip. If you decide to take a trip and you go away as soon as you make the decision, your excitement may not last long. Instead, if you decide to take the trip, make the booking, but wait for a few weeks or even months before you actually go. You build anticipation, energy, excitement, and motivation to do all the things you have always wanted.

If you find inspiration and want to go after a goal, don't start right away. Set a date in the future, mark it on the calendar, and allow yourself to get excited about your goal while that date approaches.

28. **Commit publicly:** As our motivation comes and goes, we often have to take drastic measures to make sure we follow through with our commitment and we will be accountable for not doing what we said we will do. When we commit

publicly we put ourselves in a space we cannot back up, simply because we do not want to look bad in front of others. Announce publicly what you intend to do – this may be on your Facebook page, a company meeting, or a family gathering. Then hold yourself accountable and commit to accomplish what you said you will do. The expectation to succeed now is coming not only from you, but also from others.

29. **Think about your goal every day:** When something is out of sight, it is out of mind. Make your goal just a few words long, like a mantra ("Exercise 15 minutes. Daily"), and make it visible by posting your goal on your wall in your bedroom or on your refrigerator, by saving it as wallpaper on your smartphone, or by emailing it to yourself and receiving it as a daily reminder. There are many other things you can do to make your goal visible – the most important thing you need to remember is your goal has to be at the top of your mind and visual cues should act as a constant reminder of what you need to accomplish. When you think and take small steps every day toward your goal, your goal will almost certainly become true.

30. **Decide in advance how you will deal with low motivation, and never give up:** As your motivation comes and goes, you need to develop a plan as to what you will do when your motivation is low or nonexistent. This plan will help you deal easily with those difficult moments without having to make any decisions. When we make decisions, we reduce the reserves of our energy; this is something you want to avoid when it is not necessary. When your motivation is low, all you have to do is follow through with your plan. The plan

may include different approaches such as: to think of the end result and how you will feel when you accomplish your goal, to call your mentor, to ask for advice and support, or simply to get some rest and re-energize. In any case do not give up going after your goal for any reason. Stick with it and your motivation will return.

31. **Read about your goal on a daily basis:** When we read anything related to our goal, we stay focused and increase our motivation. Make it a daily habit to read books, magazines, blogs, articles, biographies, success stories, or anything else related to your goal. Following this tactic is extremely important especially those days you feel unmotivated and you need an extra boost.

32. **Stretch past your limits on a daily basis:** I read somewhere that "walking the old, familiar paths is how you grow old"; I couldn't agree more. By testing and stretching your limits every day, you have opportunity to grow and evolve. When you stay on the same course, you do not know what you are able to accomplish and what is next for you. High performance athletes stretch their own limits every day and this is why they are so good at what they do.

33. **Ask for support when your motivation is low:** Our motivation levels are not always the same. There are times we feel we can accomplish anything; other times we just want to give up! You need to realize this is a normal thing that happens to everyone. When our motivation is low, we should not be afraid we may look weak asking help from people who love and support us. Share your thoughts and fears with others; ask for their point of

view and support. People are eager to help us as long as we give them the opportunity.

34. **Think about the benefits, not difficulties:** When we have difficult things to do, we tend to doubt ourselves and think how difficult the task will be, rather than focusing on what we will get at the end of it. When you really want something, it is a given you may need to put a lot of effort to accomplish it. Letting those difficulties control your thoughts should not be an option. While you are tackling your goals, focus on the end result – not the difficulties of the present moment. This is what will motivate you and keep you going.

35. **Replace negative thoughts with positive thoughts – every time:** Monitor your thoughts, recognize the thoughts that hold you back; replace them with positive ones. While the process may be challenging sometimes, the positive thoughts are what will help you achieve what you want. Replacing your negative thoughts should become a habit and practiced on a daily basis [14].

36. **Make it fun:** When we are happy, we enjoy what we are doing; everything seems much easier. One of the things you can do when you want to increase your motivation, is to make the journey towards your goal fun and exciting.

Before you even start working on your goal, ask yourself [15]:

• How can I enjoy this task?

• What can I do to make this task memorable, fun, and exciting?

- How can I make this task fun for others?

- How can I make this the best part of my day?

At the end, it is all about attitude, our own perspective and how we see things. If you start your day on the wrong foot, as we say, then everything may possibly go wrong until the moment you change your own attitude and how you see things. It is true though you may not manage to like some tasks, as much as you try. As long as you have genuinely tried, let it be. Do the unpleasant tasks first; get them out of the way then focus on the tasks you have found good reasons to enjoy.

37. **Reward yourself:** One of the easiest and most powerful ways of motivating yourself is by making an agreement to reward yourself at the end of an accomplished result. Break the goal into milestones and reward yourself every time you reach one. Here are some examples of agreements you can make with yourself. At the end of an accomplished result you may reward yourself by: taking a 10 minute break, eating the food you like, spending a day without doing any work, buying new clothes, etc.; choose a reward you would really enjoy and you will anticipate receiving it.

38. **Acknowledge and celebrate your failures:** It can be difficult to admit failure, but acknowledging it creates the opportunity to reflect and try to understand what went wrong. We can use what we learned from our failures as lessons to achieve bigger and better goals. Redefine your failures as feedback and as a natural part of a successful life. Michael Jordan once said "I've missed more than 9000 shots in my career. I've lost

almost 300 games. 26 times, I've been trusted to make the game winning shot and missed. I've failed over and over and over again in my life. And that is why I succeed."

39. **Take success seriously, but not seriously enough:** Don't use success as the ultimate way to achieve happiness. Highly successful people are not always happy, and success comes and goes. Get excited and seek success but don't let this define who you are. If you are not successful by other people's standards, doesn't mean you are not accomplished in your own way.

40. **Don't wait for perfection. Take action now:** Perfection can be costly and doesn't always serve our purpose. I know many examples of business owners who delayed launching their new business because they wanted to wait and create the ideal conditions. In the meantime, their competitors launched earlier – even though everything was not perfect, they were learning as they were going –they ended up with a large market share, just by launching first.

41. **No Regrets:** The desire not to have any regrets in life – personal or professional – is a reason that motivates many of us. People don't want to live with any regrets and thus are motivated to not disappoint themselves.

42. **Find out what is stopping you:** Sometimes the best way to motivate ourselves is to identify what is stopping us. By identifying, isolating, analyzing, and then removing the problem(s) we can increase our motivation. Is it fear, lack of available time, being tired, or the fact you are lazy that is stopping you? In addition, to so many other reasons, hidden

fears, and anxieties can keep you from getting things done. No matter what the reason, identify, and deal with it rather than ignoring it and letting it become a constant problem.

43. **Get the Right Tools:** Computers that are too slow, software or hardware that doesn't work as it should, a vehicle that breaks down often, and anything else you are using as a tool to accomplish your goals that doesn't perform, can kill your motivation. You need to avoid the traps that can stop motivation, as it is as important as building motivation. Having the right tools that support your goals is crucial, especially when you can save a lot of time and frustration.

44. **Five minutes rule:** When you find it difficult to motivate yourself to work on a task, commit yourself to work for only five minutes. Once you start, then it will be easy to keep on going.

45. **Plan your day, and do the toughest things first:** Get up early every day and do all the important tough things early in the morning. This will ease a lot of your day-to-day worries and boost your self-confidence for the rest of the day. Building momentum early in the day usually carries you forward [16].

46. **There are no small problems:** Small problems that create constant frustration can kill your motivation. Deal with those small problems as if they are big ones, or they will kill any drive and motivation you have [17].

47. **Get out of your comfort zone:** Facing your challenges increases motivation. When we face what intimidates us, and

eventually conquer it, it gives us a feeling we can accomplish anything; that boosts our motivation.

48. **Build on a blank canvas:** Past experiences often limit our imagination, the way we view our life and our future, and often decrease our motivation. We need to start from scratch and imagine we are painting our future on a blank canvas. When you create the future from nothing, you will realize your possibilities are much bigger than what you think. Just use your imagination and creativity and think outside of the box, as to what you think is possible. Write down your ideas and everything that will motivate and inspire you.

49. **Educate yourself, and do research on what you are about to accomplish:** Education and research helps us get a better understanding of our goal and what we are about to accomplish. This will give us the opportunity to discover the real challenges we have to face and find out what others have done in similar situations. Then we can use their examples and lessons for our benefit. When we understand something, we reduce the fear of what used to be the unknown. Without fear we can see the real possibilities and this increases our motivation.

50. **Compare yourself with yourself; not with others:** Comparing yourself with others can kill your motivation; you don't actually get any benefit from doing this. Some may be miles ahead of you in some fields in their life, yet may be seriously behind in others. You have to focus on your own results, and your own circumstances and accomplishments. The first thing you need to do is identify and acknowledge your accomplishments. When you do that, the results may

pleasantly surprise you, as you will have the opportunity to see how far you have come. Positive results motivate you to go after other goals.

51. **Make deals with yourself:** A simple trick to overcome procrastination and increase motivation is by making deals with yourself. The format is as follows:

If I accomplish X, then Y reward will happen.

As an example: If I study for 3 hours, then I can go for a walk in the park, or If I diet for 5 days, then I will have my favorite dessert.

52. **Every morning write down the things you are grateful for:** When we are grateful for things we already have, we start our day on a positive uplifting tone; this motivates us to go after other things we also want to accomplish.

Motivational Techniques

Inspired from the book "Feeling Good: The New Mood Therapy Revised and Updated", by Dr. David Burns, this is summary [18] of twelve motivational techniques that deal with various situations and will help you take action:

1. **Technique** to improve negative assumptions **(Anti-procrastination Sheet)**

   When to use: You can use the technique for any activity you've been avoiding because you think it will be difficult and unrewarding.

The Approach: Break the activity into small steps; predict the difficulty and your satisfaction VS actual activity and actual satisfaction on a scale of 100.

The goal: When you do this technique you will realize that on a scale of 100, the actual difficulty will be much less than you predicted, and the actual satisfaction will be much higher than what you anticipated.

2. **Technique** to deal with excuses **(Butt-Rebuttal Method)**

When to use: Use the technique if excuses get in the way of doing things.

The Approach: Write down the task you want to accomplish. Raise the first reason that comes to mind for not wanting to accomplish the task and use the word BUT. Example: "I want to go running, BUT it's a hot day". The next step is to write a statement that cancels the previous statement. Example "I know that it is too hot, BUT I will run by the water and it will be cooler".

The goal: By using this technique and the power of the word "BUT", the ultimate goal is to continue the process until you've run out of excuses.

3. **Technique** to fight your fear of failure **(Can't Lose System)**

When to use: Use this technique to deal with situations where you want to accomplish something important to you, but you do not proceed because you fear you will fail.

The Approach: This is a four step strategy: a) Write down your worst case fears, b) Make a list of the things that can happen if you fail, c) Look at your fears objectively and identify how real they are, d) Identify coping strategies in the case your fears are real.

The goal: This is a great technique because you put things into perspective, and you can see if your fears are real, or you blow things out of proportion. By identifying coping strategies in advance, you set up a plan for dealing with failure. This is half of the battle when fighting your fears.

4. **Technique** to remind yourself of the positive actions you take each day and improve your self-confidence **(Count What Counts)**

   When to use: Use this technique when you want to remind yourself of all the positive actions you take every day to inspire yourself to achieve new goals and help improve your self-confidence.

   The Approach: This is a very simple, yet effective technique. Every time you do something positive, track it. You can use a notebook, your smartphone, or anything else to help you keep track.

   The goal: The idea behind this technique is counting your positive actions, you train your brain to notice and value your positive actions. Over time you will notice your positive actions are increasing (one reason is you are noticing more of them) and this help you increase your confidence.

5. **Technique** to stop procrastinating and take action **(Daily Activity Schedule)**

    When to use: Use this technique when you feel you are in a vicious circle of procrastination and you want to get out of it.

    The Approach: For this simple and effective technique, you need to schedule your day and record in each time slot, what you actually did during the day. Then you identify which activities are for mastery or pleasure. The last step is to rate each pleasure activity from 0 – 5, where 0 is low and 5 is high, and each mastery activity from 0 – 5, where 0 is very easy and 5 is very difficult.

    The goal: This technique helps you find the joy in things you do every day, and refocuses you on simple pleasures and mastery in doing things.

6. **Technique** to respond to pushy critics with advice **(Disarming Technique)**

    When to use: This technique helps you deal with critics who even though may give you great advice, you feel are trying to push you around.

    The Approach: This technique works when you genuinely listen to your critics; disarm them in a way you show you agree with them – not because this is what they want or expect from you, but because this is your decision.

    The goal: This disarming technique helps you deal with your critics by agreeing with them, yet you let them know you make your own decisions based on what you feel is right for you.

7. **Technique** to eliminate "musts", "shoulds", and "oughts" (**Motivation Without Coercion**)

   When to use: Use this technique when you feel overwhelmed by activities you feel you "must", "should", and "ought" to do.

   The Approach: Every time you have an activity you "must", "should" or "ought" to do, replace these words with "WANT". The concept behind it is to create a process that motivates you and excites you, rather than holding you back, stressing and frustrating you.

   The goal: This is an effective approach to remind yourself of what you "want to" do and why. The intention is to produce feelings of freedom of choice, personal dignity, and creating positive action towards your goals.

8. **Technique** to find out what activities you really enjoy and how much you enjoy them (**Pleasure Predicting Sheet**)

   When to use: To find out what activities you really enjoy doing.

   The Approach: This is a three step process: a) Write down the list of activities you will do for pleasure. b) Predict your satisfaction on a 100 point scale, before you do the activity. c) After, record your actual satisfaction.

   The goal: The goal is to find out the activities you really enjoy doing, and to eliminate the ones that are time wasters and do not make you happy.

9. **Technique** to endorse yourself **(Self-Endorsement)**

    When to use: Use this technique when you beat yourself for things you haven't accomplished or actions you haven't taken.

    The Approach: Write down a list of your self-downing statements. Then next to each statement write your self-endorsing statements. The key part is to mention and focus on your accomplishments. Example:

    > Self-downing statement: I cleaned my room, but it's not as clean as it should be.

    > Self-endorsing statement: The room is much cleaner than it was yesterday.

    > Accomplishment: I have a heavy schedule with work, school, and other activities/priorities, yet I managed to find time to clean the room. I did a great job!

    The goal: The key is to lift yourself up, endorse yourself, and get the motivation to move forward with your goals.

10. **Technique** to test your negative assumptions **(Test Your Can't-s)**

    When to use: Use this technique when you feel you have a pattern of thinking that tells you constantly "I can't do this", or "I can't do that", and you keep on discouraging yourself.

The Approach: The concept is simple. Rather than just think you can't do something, prove you can. Instead of testing the big picture and overwhelming yourself, break down your assumptions into small hurdles. Then take action and test against each one, proving yourself right or wrong.

The goal: The goal is to put your negative thoughts into test. Is it true you really cannot do something or you think you cannot do it?

11. **Technique** for getting past negative thoughts that block you from taking action **(TIC-TOC Technique)**

When to use: Use this technique when you have negative thoughts that prevent you from taking action.

The Approach: Write down the negative thoughts that stop you. The next step is to evaluate each thought objectively. Are your thoughts valid or ideas built on previous thought patterns? Then list thoughts that can help you either defeat the negative thoughts or provide a positive action. The last step is to replace the negative thoughts with the positive ones. You may want to use some of the techniques I discussed above.

The goal: The goal is to prevent negative thoughts from stopping you when you want to take action.

12. **Technique** for visualizing Success

When to use: Visualizing success is a great motivation technique and you can use it every time you want to push yourself in accomplishing a goal.

The Approach: This is a four step process: a) Get a good picture of the end result in mind, b) List the advantages of taking positive action, c) Fantasize you have already accomplished your goal. Imagine how it would feel. d) Go through your list of benefits one by one. State each benefit as if you already have it. For example, "now that I have more clients, I don't have to work as hard to build new business".

The goal: When we visualize success, we can focus on the benefits and what we really want. The constant reminder of success will motivate us to take action and move us closer to our goal.

CHAPTER 21

TOOLS AND THINGS TO DO TO KEEP YOU ORGANIZED AND MOTIVATED

Throughout this book I present concepts, methods, and ideas that can help get things done and get you closer to your goal. Practical tricks, tools, and techniques are important as well since they keep you organized and motivated, while they help you stay focused and save a lot of your time. Chose the tools and techniques that best serve your purpose:

Tools to use:

Mind Maps: A mind map is a diagram used to visually organize information. It is a visual thinking tool that helps structure information and helps you to better analyze, comprehend, synthesize, recall, and generate new ideas. A mind map is drawn as an image in the center of a blank landscape page, to which associated representations of ideas such as images, words and parts of words are added. The power of mind maps lies in their simplicity [1].

You can create your mind map on a paper, but there are also some great online mind maps such as "MindMeister" [2].

Create a detailed action plan: Action plans are very important because they help us set up achievable milestones for our goals, and organize our day to day activities. You need to create two types of plans:

1. A Master Action Plan lets you set up your goals, objectives, milestones, and an evaluation system from the start until the accomplishment of your goal.

2. A Weekly Action Plan lets you set up your weekly activities. Each time you reach your short term goals and your weekly plan ends, you prepare the plan for the next week.

Online Calendar: A very simple and common, yet very effective tool, a calendar lets you to keep your life organized. Once you set activities in your Calendar, you do not have to worry about them. You let your calendar decide what is for you to do next, and you just go about your business.

Online calendars are an excellent tool for time management and they can be accessed from any device that can connect to the internet (desktops, tablets, and smartphones). This is extremely useful since it is impossible to forget or lose (unlike a physical planner), and can help you keep your life on track.

Another unique benefit of online calendars is you can easily share your calendar with others. If you have permission, you can view the calendar of others and invite anyone to meetings and events. This makes coordination much more effective than having to contact each individual about tasks written into a personal planner.

Google Calendar is my calendar of choice; it allows me to keep life organized easily, intuitively, with no hassle or slow interface. These are some of its benefits:

a. It's free

b. Easy to use and the interface is fast

c. You can sync your calendar with your phone or tablet

d. You can share your calendar with others, and if you have permission, you can see the calendar of others

e. You can subscribe to numerous pre-populated calendars for free

f. It is integrated with Gmail and you can create events on your calendar right from an email

g. You can set up notifications and reminders

h. It is searchable

• **Create a Status Report**: A status report helps keep track of important events, conversations, activities, and determines the next steps, type of action, and who is involved. Always keep your status report up to date. I update my own status report multiple times during a day.

• **Reminders:** Send, through Google Calendar, email, or other online tools, reminders to yourself to bring to your attention all important activities and events you should not forget.

• **Write things down:** Your mind doesn't like loose ends;

writing things down keeps you organized and focused. Instead of thinking "what do I have to do next?", or "I should not forget this", writing things down lets you know what is the next thing to do.

- **Notepad:** Keep with you all the time a notepad, a sheet of paper, or any other system you can use to record anything that comes to mind. Important thoughts and ideas can come as "hatches" and we need to record them so we will not forget them. Another benefit for doing this is that by writing our thoughts, we give them a substance and we make them real.

- **Use a To-Do priority list:** Manage your day by creating a to-do list. Long lists are usually unmanageable; they stress us and are not completed. Focus on three key items per day. Usually completing **three key items** means the day has been productive. Prioritize the three items from the most important to the less important. Only when you complete the three items, do you continue on to other projects. Reorganise your list, if for any reason priorities change.

- **Keep a goal card:** Write down your goal on a card; keep it always with you and read it many times throughout the day. Goal cards help us stay focused, especially when things do not always go our way [3].

- **Whiteboard:** Keep visual cues of your goals and the important-to-do-tasks on a whiteboard or in places that are easy to see. This can be a whiteboard in your office or your bedroom, even a note on the mirror of your washroom. Those visual reminders will keep top of mind what is important to you.

- **Note cards:** Use note cards to write tasks on (one task per card) or in a list. The stack of note cards becomes an easy prioritization tool. They can be used as placeholders, as mini-white boards, and as tokens to model ideas. They are easy to carry around and attach to other documents. In addition, different colors allow a visual representation of different kinds of to-do's. Note cards are affordable and easy to reconfigure as needs and projects change [4].

- **Read, Watch, Listen:** Become a lifelong student, read personal development books, watch inspirational videos, listen to motivational speakers, and continue growing. Reading informative books (and comprehending them) is another good way to exercise the cognitive efficiency of your prefrontal cortex. Even 15 minutes of inspirational content on Monday morning can set up your day and your week for success.

  Some of the books you may want to check out [5]:

  Infinite Self by Stuart Wilde

  The Power Of Now by Eckhart Tolle

  Awaken The Giant Within by Anthony Robbins

  Manifesting Change by Mike Dooley

  The Success Principles by Jack Canfield

  You Are A Badass by Jen Sincero

  The Secret by Rhonda Byrne

- **Review new knowledge within 24 hours:** Review what you learned within 24 hours since it will increase retention by 80%.

- **Use tools to eliminate temptations and distractions:** We often allow distractions such as reading our emails or visiting social media many times a day take us away from our goal. Identify those distractions and develop a plan to eliminate them. One example is using *Freedom*, an internet blocking productivity software. www.macfreedom.com

Techniques, methods and principles to use:

- **Use the IF X, then Y technique:**

This simple, yet effective technique, can been successful for any goal you can think of, personal or professional, and of any size. This technique is based on the following formula:

If X happens, then I will do Y.

Visit Chapter 16 to read more about this technique.

- **Use the Pomodoro Time Management Technique:**

This technique [6] helps us stay focused on a task during the set time, and increases our productivity and energy levels. There are five basic steps to implementing the technique:

1. Decide on the task to be done

2. Set the Pomodoro timer to *n* minutes (traditionally 25)

3. Work on the task until the timer rings; record with an *x*

4. Take a short break (3–5 minutes)

5. After four Pomodori, take a longer break (15–30 minutes)

- **Use Pareto's Principle:**

A very well-known principle [7], it says that 20% input gives 80% output.

Pareto's Principle, the 80/20 Rule, should serve as a daily reminder to focus 80 percent of your time and energy on the 20 percent of your work that is really important. Don't just "work smart", work smart on the right things. For that reason, we should focus on doing the 20% of the most difficult tasks at the very beginning of the day. While you are doing this, avoid multitasking as it can cost you 40% efficiency.

- **Use the Eisenhower Method:**

To motivate yourself on a daily basis, you must set goals and monitor them on a daily basis. A good tool to use is the Eisenhower Method. The "Eisenhower Method" stems from a quote attributed to Dwight D. Eisenhower: "I have two kinds of problems, the urgent and the important. The urgent are not important, and the important are never urgent."

This is how it works and how you can prioritize your goals:

a. Take a blank sheet of paper and draw a large square on

it. Divide the square into four quadrants. The left hand side column gets the label name "Urgent" and the right hand side column, the label name "Not Urgent". The top row gets the label name "Important" and the bottom row, the label name "Not Important".

b. The first upper left quadrant contains the tasks that are urgent and important. These are tasks you have to do or else you will face negative consequences. Examples are: medical emergencies, filing your taxes on the set date, etc.

c. The second upper right quadrant contains important and not urgent tasks. Tasks in quadrant two are in direct alignment with your goals and things you want to achieve in the long-run. This is the quadrant you want to invest most of your time. Examples are: working on your business while maintaining your current job, exercising, spending time with friends and family.

d. The third lower left quadrant contains tasks that are not important yet urgent. Often called the quadrant of deception, this quadrant includes everything we think is urgent and important but actually isn't. While we often shift our focus to these tasks, the reality is they are just sources of distraction and do not help us directly achieve our goals. These tasks should actually belong in quadrant four. Examples: picking up your phone while you are working, checking your Facebook updates, constantly checking your email inbox, responding right away to people on instant messenger, or checking your phone for text messages.

e. The fourth lower right quadrant contains tasks that are not important and not urgent, are time wasters, and you want to avoid as much as possible. Examples: following the news, playing video games, watching reruns of your favorite TV shows. As it is really important to have a balanced life between work and your personal life, you should not eliminate the tasks and activities in this quadrant. The challenge is to allocate most of your time to quadrant two, with just enough of time spent in quadrant four to get by.

This is what the Eisenhower Method [8] looks like:

	URGENT	NOT URGENT
IMPORTANT	Crying Baby Kitchen Fire	Exercise Vacation Planning
NOT IMPORTANT	Interruptions Distractions Other Calls	Trivia Time Wasters
The four-quadrant "Eisenhower Decision Matrix" for importance and urgency		

Better planning and giving higher priority to things that matter most allows you to make better decisions, balance work and life better, and live a more abundant life. Focusing on Quadrant 2 activities, using time found by eliminating Quadrant 4 activities, can make all the difference in what you can accomplish in life [9].

Practical tips to increase your motivation and performance:

- Develop an accountability system that takes away your ability to procrastinate and make excuses and that makes you stick to your plan and highest values. Ask others to hold you accountable and keep in constant communication with them. Find a working buddy or people who have the same goals, find and talk to mentors who have been there and done that, work side-by-side with a co-worker (or friend), hire a coach, join (or create) a mastermind group, or use the website www.stickk.com.

- Set up a power day. This is a day you are committed to get things done. You are determined to stay focused and avoid any type of distraction that prevents you from doing what you said you will do. In the same context, you can set a power hour or power morning. As long as we set aside a block of time to get things done, and we follow through, then our goal is accomplished.

- Always plan ahead, and be proactive. Planning ahead and religiously following through on your plan, is very important to move forward. You can use planning for challenging tasks and activities or for simple ones such as planning your meals in advance. Being proactive though is equally important if you want to avoid delays and frustration. If you are a hiring manager for your firm and you know your company is growing rapidly, if you do not work in advance to find the people you may need, then you are not proactive. If you know the birthday of your wife or husband is coming and you leave it to the last minute to buy a gift – and you cannot find exactly what you want – this is a result of you not being proactive.

- Delegate as much as you can. Learning to delegate is a big step if you want to accomplish a lot of things within a short of period of time. When there is someone who can do the task better and faster than you, then it is time to delegate, and for you to focus on the things that matter and only you can do. There is no reason to spread yourself thin and do every little thing yourself.

- Treat time like money. Many people do not understand the value of their time and they waste it doing unproductive things they want to do, or they let it pass without taking full advantage of it. Time is precious and you need to respect your time and demand from others to respect your time as well.

- Run every task through an impact vs. effort analysis. You do not want to spend a lot of time and effort, for a task that will have the least impact in helping you move faster toward your goal. Always ask to find the task that requires the least amount of effort, and produces the highest result.

- Build self-awareness through monitoring. This is about consciously being aware of what you are doing each day, and is linked with self-control. Most people have little idea how much time they spend online, how much they eat, and how much money they spend. When we do not know exactly where we are, it is difficult to know what we have achieved, what we need to change, and determine how far we need to go.

We need to develop a monitoring system where we gather and then analyze information about our life. Use apps that track how much time you spend online, keep a food diary of what you eat each day, and so on. The clearer the reminders you have of both your progress and backsliding, the easier it will be to stay on track.

- Avoid being a perfectionist. One of the reasons you may be struggling to stay organized and getting things done, is you spend way too much time on one task. This leaves no time for other things you had to do that day [10].

- Embrace and appreciate what you have already accomplished. Take the opportunity to reward yourself for a job well done.

- Believe in yourself no matter what. If you do not truly believe in yourself, the probability is no one else will.

- Wake up early in the morning (as early as 5:00 a.m.), to have time to do the things you want to accomplish within the day. This is the perfect time to organize in your mind the things you need to do within the day, and do some of the must do activities that will help you start your day in a happy place and are considered small victories (example: exercise). When you achieve a series of small victories, the boost in your confidence can last for months.

- Do not be afraid of criticism. Accept and welcome criticism since often it helps us grow and become better in what we do.

- Say "no" more often; especially to temptation taking you away from your goals.

- Be grateful for all the things you have in your life, no matter how big or small they are.

- Declare your plans to others. When you declare your plans, you show others how serious you are about the things you want to accomplish and internally you are making a commitment you are going to follow through.

- Do not be afraid of failure. Failure is part of the process of becoming successful; it happens to everyone including those considered very successful. Learn from your mistakes and move forward no matter what.

- Be consistent with your efforts, or anything else you do. If you are working hard one day and another day you are slacking and wasting your time, you lack consistency. Every day you need to do something that takes you closer to your end goal.

- Do not be lazy. If you truly want to accomplish your goals, then being lazy is the last thing you should do. You should be eager to do the necessary work required, and go above and beyond to accomplish what you want.

- Use your imagination, and allow originality and creativity to become part of who you are. Encourage yourself to be creative and open to new ideas and concepts, as this can help you find solutions to existing problems and eventually grow.

- Let new ideas grow and mature. Take the time to process a new idea and allow it to grow in your mind. When you have a new idea it is possible not all the pieces are aligned.

When we let an idea grow, we see things we didn't see before. We can adjust it to serve our purpose in the best possible way.

- Be a team player, and avoid playing it solo. You can accomplish much more with the help, support, and encouragement of others.

- Tackle issues right way. Sometimes it is easier and faster to tackle an issue right away rather than letting it stay at the back of your mind and delaying action for a later time. Apply the same principle when you are receiving emails you can deal with and reply right away.

- Meet Face-to-Face or have a conference call. We often waste a lot of time exchanging emails, when an issue can be solved within a few minutes, with a conference call or meeting face-to-face.

- Avoid distractions. Distractions take many forms, and you need to avoid them at all costs. As an example, it is really easy when you are working on a project to visit websites like Facebook, and what you might intend as a 5 minute break can turn into losing hours of valuable work time. These are some of the things you can do to avoid distractions:

  a. Check and answer your emails only once or twice a day, at a set time.

  b. Turn off email notifications.

  c. Do not answer phone calls unless the person on the other line has an appointment to talk to you right at that moment; this will cut down on distractions, and derailing your day.

d. Use tools that can help you reduce distractions. One example is the free extension for Chrome called Block Site. This extension will prevent you from visiting websites while you are working.

e. Inform others you are going to be busy working on a task, and set up a time when you will be available for them.

- Delete it, don't re-schedule it [11]. You need to be realistic about what is important and needs to be done. If you have a task on your list you keep re-scheduling; you need to ask yourself if the task should be there. We usually re-schedule again and again because we do not see urgency. Something we have in our to-do list, that seemed important, might not be important any more. You should feel comfortable with deleting anything no longer relevant.

- Stay on top of your health. When we are sick, we are unable to do all the things we want to accomplish. Taking care of yourself and your health is very important and one of the best investments you can make. Devote time to manage your health, eat healthy, and exercise.

- Create a sustainable routine. Often when you try too hard (example: working long hours) you end up burning out. On the other hand, when we do not put enough effort, we do not get things done. You need to plan your day, and create a sustainable routine that will support all the things you want to do within your day. Plan all the activities that are important and you do every day. How many hours you will work, what time you will eat, plan the time you will spend with friends and family members, etc.

- Always set deadlines. When you do not set deadlines, other seemingly more important priorities may appear. The result is you may end up delaying what you initially set out to do. Don't be afraid to set deadlines for everything you need to do. Deadlines keep us on track and help us fulfil our commitments to ourselves and others.

- Always prioritize the things that must happen without forgetting to review your action plan and identify priorities you might have forgotten to include.

- Never procrastinate. Often, looking back, we regret things we haven't done because we allowed procrastination to get the best of us. Procrastination is an enemy and taking action is the best weapon to defeat it.

- Keep moving forward and do not stop, even if you are tired. Sometimes we do not feel like doing a task, or we are very tired. Even though we do not want to burn ourselves out, we also need to push ourselves to our limits. We are more capable of accomplishing things than we think, as long as we have the will to make things happen.

- You can save a lot of time by batching your tasks. For example, check and respond to emails all at once. Make your phone calls all at once, etc.

- Get to inbox zero every day. By doing this, you will not have loose ends and, things will not occupy your mind; you can start your next day fresh.

•   Do the one thing that would make you satisfied with your day. Identify one thing that will make your day a success, block the necessary time, and do it.

•   Write down your thoughts. Writing is a way to help process things. It clears your mind of thoughts that would otherwise sap your energy and provides a sounding board for ideas.

•   Develop a thinking schedule: Thinking is a discipline. If you want to be better at developing new ideas, evaluate your views and accomplishments, and figure out where you want to go, you need to set aside the time that best suits you, to do just that.

•   Set fun activities: When you set up fun activities outside the hard to do tasks, you motivate yourself to finish on time and meet your deadlines. While you may work hard, you also need the time to rest and enjoy.

•   Mirror and imitate successful people. According to Wikipedia, mirroring is a behavior where an individual **subconsciously imitates the gesture, speech pattern, or attitude of another**. Mirroring usually happens in social situations, including events with friends or colleagues, family gatherings, etc. Mirroring can establish rapport with the individual who is being mirrored, as similarities in nonverbal gestures allow the individual to feel more connected with the person exhibiting the mirrored behavior. As the two individuals display similar nonverbal gestures, they may believe they share similar attitudes and ideas, and they feel a greater sense of engagement and belonging within the situation.

While mirroring is happening at the subconscious level, **imitation** occurs when an individual **observes and replicates another's behavior.** Imitation is also a form of social learning that leads to the "development of traditions, and ultimately our culture. It allows for the transfer of information (behaviors, customs, etc.) between individuals and through generations without the need for genetic inheritance [12].

When we constantly mirror and imitate successful people, we make their behaviors, attitudes, gestures, and speech patterns our own and part of our daily routine. These new good behaviors will help us fight back all those things that hold us back, give us a new outlook on life, and open our minds into welcoming new possibilities.

CHAPTER 22

MIRRORING AND IMITATING SUCCESSFUL PEOPLE

Success is the ability to feel fulfilled in every aspect of one's life. It is the way you view the world, and the sum of an infinite amount of tasks, wins, and failures performed while moving towards a specific direction in life. If you get to point B and you stop, you will never find out what lies ahead. For that reason, success is considered a journey and not a destination and the search for success is a never-ending process.

While everyone wants to be successful, only a small percentage of people manage to reach success in every aspect of their life.

What is it though the most successful people do different than others?

The world's most successful people have one thing in common: they think differently from everyone else. Instead of reacting to what is happening around them, they use their conscious mind (thinking mind) rather than allowing their emotions to make decisions for them, and without fear they plan ahead as to what they would like to accomplish. Successful people make a habit of doing the things unsuccessful people don't want to do [1,2].

Mirroring and imitating highly successful people will get you into the habit of doing some of the good habits they do and may apply to your situation. Here are some habits of highly successful people:

They are fearless: Successful people recognize the difference between fear and danger. While danger is real, they know fear is a lasting emotion fueled by imagination and a choice. Instead of letting their fears take over, they challenge them and get satisfaction by conquering them.

They are not afraid to make mistakes: They see mistakes as an opportunity to learn and grow.

They think positive: Successful people monitor their thinking allowing only positive thoughts to enter their mind. This positive outlook and attitude creates a space where it is easier for them to recognize new opportunities and make things happen.

They use positive body language: Successful people use positive language techniques such as: positive gestures and expressions, an enthusiastic tone of voice, they uncross their arms, they maintain eye contact, and they lean towards the person who's speaking to draw others in. Positive body language makes all the difference in a conversation because how you say something can be more important than what you say.

They leave a strong first impression: Successful people know most people decide whether or not they will like them within the first seven seconds of meeting. For that reason they make sure they leave a great first impression. First impressions are tied intimately to positive body language. A strong posture, a firm handshake, a smile, and open shoulders help ensure your first impression is a great one.

They speak assertively: They know to get people to listen. They present their ideas with conviction. They avoid expressions that indicate they are not in control of what they are talking about like "I'm not sure", or "I think".

They are grateful: Highly successful people recognize others for the amazing things they have done for them and their contribution to their success including, their mentors, colleagues, families, and friends.

They avoid negative energy: Successful people not only have a positive outlook in life but they also avoid, to the best of their abilities, letting anyone with negative energy enter their life. Those who do not support them, try to take advantage of them, are jealous of their success, and have an overall negative attitude, are not welcome.

They focus on what matters: Successful people prioritize activities and focus on the important things that need to be done. When they are done, they use the remaining time to do all the other things they enjoy.

They don't have endless To-Do lists: Long lists are hard to manage and they get overwhelming. Successful people focus on their top 3 priorities for the day and when they are done, they move to other important things.

They believe in themselves: Often they do not know how they are going to accomplish a goal, but they know they can do it. They have the determination, patience, and willpower to make anything they set in their mind happen. They believe, not because they feel it is their destiny to be successful, but because they know as long as they are breathing, they will continue to work towards where they want to be and they will overcome every difficulty presented to them.

They develop their thoughts: They have the patience and they understand it takes time for an idea to fully develop and reach its full potential. Don't just settle on the first thing that comes to mind. Thoughts need to be "shaped until they have substance" and need to stand the test of "clarity and questioning."

They are not afraid to be different: They understand being different is actually a positive thing and a quality that can help them move closer to their goal. They acknowledge popular thinking does not always lead to the expected results, so they are willing to take risks to get the results they want. In addition, they appreciate themselves for who they are and their uniqueness.

They stand for what they believe, no matter what: They are willing to take a stand for their ideas and beliefs no matter what the situation, and they are willing to put themselves at risk and go against anyone who does not agree with them.

They go all in: Successful people are willing to risk everything and give themselves 100% to what they believe in. It doesn't always pay off, but they know they have done their best; and when it does pay off, it pays huge dividends.

They learn from their failures: Successful people always step back from projects after all is said and done, look at the results, and learn from their failures. They often call it the school of life. They know by trial and error they can get better and avoid the same mistakes in the future. They understand the only thing that can stop from trying again is themselves.

They embrace difficulties: Those who are successful, are considered problem solvers. They enjoy finding solutions for life's challenges, they lead by example, and are willing to face anything that comes their way.

They follow through: Their word is very important to them. If they say they will do something, they mean it, and they will make sure they follow through.

They support others and are willing to mentor: They see a higher purpose in helping others to achieve their goals and they believe the more successful people there are, the better the world will be. They are willing to donate their time, skills, wealth, and knowledge to others for the better good, and during the process, they stay modest. They have no problem taking someone under their wing and showing them the path they should take to achieve their goals. They do not feel threatened by the young and ambitious, instead, they believe they must guide the new generations as they will become the future. While human beings are programmed with a survival of the fittest mentality, only by fighting greed and helping others can you truly reach success.

They control their thoughts and emotions: Unsuccessful people live in the past, allowing pain and emotional trauma to control their lives. They relive what happened in the past, again and again, rather than focusing on the present. Successful people have the ability to control their thoughts and emotions, they focus on the present; they have a positive attitude regardless of the circumstances.

They are graceful: Graceful people are the perfect combination of strong and gentle. They're approachable, likeable, and easy to get along with. All these are qualities that make people highly responsive to their ideas.

They never stop learning: While many people stop learning when they are done school, the truly successful people see education and learning new things, as a way of life and they have genuine hunger for learning and obtaining knowledge. They seek opportunities to research, study, and experiment with something new every day. They are not afraid to read, watch, or listen to things that are different, that may expand their knowledge and their understanding of the world. As technology has evolved over the years, the access to huge amounts of information has made their thirst for knowledge even bigger and their chances to succeed further even greater.

Successful people have a purpose: Their purpose – their larger than life goal and passion – is what drives them every day and motivates them to use their time wisely, to avoid procrastination and distractions, and to develop feasible short- and long-term plans. They know what they want to gain, where they intend on going, and they have their course drawn out.

They are deliberate: Successful people make decisions by taking the time to think things out, they seek advice from others, and they sleep on it. They know they are ineffective when they make decisions on their gut feelings.

They remain humble: Highly successful people do not take their success for granted. They know it was not luck that brought them to success, but hard, yet smart work, and determination. They never forget where they came from and how they began, and they celebrate their triumphs with modesty rather than bragging and making others uncomfortable.

They use the 80/20 Rule: The Pareto Principle is that 80% of your results (example: sales) come from 20% of your efforts (example: clients). Successful people identify that 20%, and they focus on it. While you are doing this, avoid multitasking as it can cost you 40% efficiency.

They meditate: Meditation is key with successful people. They take between 5 and 30 minutes a day to clear their mind and set the day off on the right foot. Since our mind is overwhelmed with information, meditation helps to clear the mind and cut through all of the noise.

They bounce new ideas off other people: Instead of keeping their ideas a secret, they share their thoughts with others and they ask their opinions. Colleagues, friends, industry insiders, or even strangers, can provide them feedback and often help them see something they have never thought of before.

They collaborate with others: Successful people understand by working with others, they can add additional value to their project, make it even better, and have a greater possibility for success. This is why brainstorming sessions are so effective. They evaluate their plans, research and find the right partners, and are not afraid to take the first step and make an irresistible offer that can benefit all parties involved.

They understand the importance of balance: Highly successful individuals understand the importance of balance in every aspect of their life, and they believe to be truly successful, they must take care of themselves physically, mentally, and spiritually. They meditate, exercise, work smart, and they cherish their time spent with loved ones.

They never compromise their integrity: Highly successful individuals believe honor, honesty, and courage are the ingredients that led them to success and they are not willing to compromise their integrity to get ahead. In addition, they know honesty allows for genuine connections with people in a way that dishonesty can't.

They know what they do not know: They understand they do not know everything, and search for people who are experts in their field; they seek their advice. They always weigh all options before starting something new they are not familiar with or understand.

They never give up: Giving up is simply not an option and they keep pressing on despite the obstacles they face. They know those obstacles are what will teach them precious life lessons that will bring them closer to success.

They never lose hope: They know if they lose hope, they will also lose the game. Hope, and the anticipation things will get better, is what drives them. Even when all odds are against them, highly successful individuals never lose hope.

They love their enemies: Highly successful individuals empathize with their enemies and try to see their point of view – even though they do not agree with them. They understand the horrible implications harboring hate in their hearts can bring into their lives. Therefore, with courage and conviction, they set out to spread love and kindness, even to those they can't get along with.

They never indulge in pity parties: Victim behavior is not for the highly successful individuals. No matter what life throws at them, highly successful individuals understand by throwing self-pity parties is not going to get them anywhere. Instead, with pride and courage, they fight back those difficulties and they see winning the battle as the only option.

They understand the value of time: Time is the one thing no human can buy and is therefore, the most precious thing of all. Highly successful individuals understand the time they have is a gift and they spend it wisely. Even when they rest, they make sure they use their time in the best possible way and every moment is enjoyed and savored.

They know when it is time to rest: Highly successful individuals understand the need to take a break, recharge, re-evaluate balance in their lives, to remain focused on their goals.

They don't have time for gossip: Highly successful individuals treat everyone with dignity and respect, honor everyone around them, and truly appreciate the gift each person brings into the world. Instead of wasting time on meaningless tasks, they prefer to spend their time to get to know others, share knowledge, and learn from their experiences.

Successful people never strive for perfection: they strive to grow their knowledge and continue to improve their skills.

Truly successful people **maintain certain habits** that keep them on a productive path. They read personal development books, watch inspirational videos, listen to motivational speakers. They never stop at any point along the way and their goals evolve and grow with them.

Successful people are able to accept and adapt to change: Change is happening all the time; successful people don't let it catch them off-guard. They plan for change, expect change, embrace change, and use change to their advantage.

Successful people are not afraid of commitment: If you want to be successful, you have to commit to things. A new job, a new partner, a new hobby, new friends, whatever it is – you need to commit and eliminate those commitment fears.

Cultivating patience: Tony Hsieh, CEO of Zappos – a very successful online retailer – was asked why more organizations are not like them. He said, "Patience." Hsieh explained most firms won't put in time to build employee morale and customer service. "It's whether you're willing to make that commitment," he said [3].

Patience is a virtue, and when you start cultivating patience, it can be a game changer — both personally and professionally. It doesn't matter what it is you want to achieve, knowing how to wait is what will lead you to success.

A successful website doesn't launch with thousands of visitors overnight and a Sports Illustrated model doesn't miraculously gain his or her physique in 24 hours. You have to start cultivating patience – each little step will take you closer to your goal.

They identify their downfalls, they show compassion, and then they take action: When we identify where we fall short, we have a real chance to improve all those things that hold us back. As many of us are our worst critics, it is not very difficult to identify what we need to improve.

The hardest part, once we identify our downfalls, is to take action and do something about them. Simply saying "I do not have the patience to do something", or "I fear I'm not good enough" will not take you anywhere. If the fear is you are not good enough, then you need to make sure you are good enough by developing your skills. If you say you are not a patient person, then you need to learn to control your emotions. We usually know the answer as to what we need to do. All we simply have to do is to take action, and just do it.

You should always remember once you identify your downfalls, you need to show compassion for yourself. It takes a lot of practice and effort to get it right, so don't allow yourself to get disappointed when the first obstacles appear. Just don't quit; keep on trying. Moving forward – even if you have to take baby steps – will take you much further than those who do not take any form of action.

They practice emotional creativity: Emotional creativity, better known as empathy, helps you relate to other people and is the backbone of success. Emotional creativity is about getting into other peoples' shoes, and seeing their point of view. Putting yourself in someone's situation is going to lead to better behavior and understanding on your part, it will help you connect with other people, and will make you a better person over all.

Emotional creativity can also work the other way around. Many successful people are socially accepted and likable because you can relate to them. There are different reasons why others can relate to a successful person including their creativity which creates an emotional connection [4].

They have self-control: They are able to monitor their emotions and they react to challenging situations with self-control. They are calm and content because they know no matter how good or bad things get, everything changes with time, and they can face any situation by adapting and adjusting.

They understand the importance of devoting time to think: When we do not devote time to think, we follow popular thinking and we follow our own patterns that are not always successful. Someone may say – but I'm thinking, I'm thinking all the time. This is about focusing on your goal and what is important to you rather than thinking what you need to do to make every day decisions that do not affect your future and what you want. Thinking and focusing on what matters is discipline and we can always get better by practice. It is advisable to create a thinking schedule where you are setting aside a few hours every week or every month to make plans and think of the issues that are important to you.

They think differently: They expose themselves to different ideas, types of people, and do different things. Exposing ourselves to different ideas and types of people is a good way to expand our minds, see new possibilities and a different point of view we did not think of before. Next time you meet someone you think you will not like, give him or her a chance. You may end up learning something that will eventually benefit you. As you can't always be right, value others, if you want them to value you, and give other peoples' opinions a chance. In addition, try to do things you wouldn't normally do. Meet new people, try new routes to work, read books you may consider boring. The key is to expose yourself to new ideas and ways of life.

They're appreciative: They take the time to slow down and appreciate everything they have accomplished. A huge amount of their positivity, determination, and motivation comes from their ability to stay grounded and appreciate all the opportunities that came their way.

They spend time with people who challenge them: Successful people are not afraid to spend time with people who challenge them and help them reach their full potential. When someone pushes you to your limits, it may not be pleasant at that moment, but the long term benefits can definitely be worth the effort.

They reject popular thinking: This is one of my favorite things successful people do, simply because I have come to understand popular thinking often means there is no thinking at all. Following others, just because you want to be socially accepted, will not always help you go where you want to go! Make your own decisions and think for yourself. This is your life! When you reject popular thinking, at times you may feel uncomfortable. That is fine. This feeling will give you an opportunity to grow.

They follow through with their ideas: Ideas have a short life and they come and go. Each one of us has many new ideas as to what we would like to do, ideas as to how to become wealthy, ideas as to how we would love to spend our time, ideas as to what we would like to accomplish and what we think will make us happy. Ideas have no substance if we are not taking action. In addition to that, if we do not write down our ideas, most possibly we will forget about them as though they have never occurred. Successful people fully take advantage of their ideas and this is one of the reasons they stand out.

They plan ahead: When you have a vague idea as to where you are and what you want to accomplish, you will get nowhere. The best thinkers, while they leave room for some spontaneity, plan ahead, and they reduce their margin of error by strategic thinking.

Strategic thinking is defined as a mental or thinking process applied by an individual in the context of achieving success in an endeavor.

When you want to accomplish a goal, you can apply strategic thinking by following the steps [5] below:

1. Ask why you want to accomplish a goal. What are your good reasons?

2. Break the goal down into smaller parts.

3. Identify the key issues.

4. Review your resources.

5. Put the right resources and people in place.

They have an agenda and they know what they want to accomplish: A lot of people do not have long term plans and they only focus on their day-to-day activities. Successful people plan ahead for their weeks, months, and long-term goals. Then they make sure to follow through with their plans and make the necessary adjustments accordingly.

In addition, they use their time wisely and they don't leave things to luck. They have a plan; they know what they want to accomplish and learn from others when they go into meetings, when they go to social events, or when they participate in activities.

Successful people practice reflective thinking: To think reflectively you have to: a) experience something, b) think about what happened, and c) learn from the experience. We think reflectively all the time, but most of the time we do not realize it. Have you ever missed the train or bus and then thought the next time you will leave from the house 10 minutes earlier? This is an example of reflective thinking. You thought about the experience and then you made the decision to do something different the next time.

Reflective thinking gives you perspective and confidence in your decision-making skills. If you are not reflecting, you are holding yourself back without realizing it. Socrates once said, "An unexamined life is not worth living."

They see possibilities, rather than limitations: Successful people see possibilities for themselves and others, even in the most difficult situations. Instead of complaining when things go wrong, they create new opportunities and use their energy in the most positive way under the circumstances. They think in in terms of "I will" and "I can", and they do not support negative self-talk.

Signs You Are Already Successful

We often dream of success, and we see it as something we may be able to accomplish in the very distant future. We do not realize each one of us is already successful in so many ways. Here are a few powerful and real reasons which prove you are already successful, even though you feel you are not right now:

1. **You have the time:** The most common excuse people use when they do not put any effort into achieving a goal is they do not have enough time. The reality though is you have as much time as you need. Think for a moment of your goal and then consider this: The President or Prime Minister of your country has exactly the same hours as you. 24 hours within a day. Yet he or she successfully manages a country. The CEO of Apple is managing a company worth over 500 billion dollars. He has exactly the same time like you within a day; 24 hours. How come these people manage to accomplish so much while you cannot devote time to your goal?

   We definitely have the time, but we choose to do only the things that are fun, are not difficult, and the ones that do not take us out of our comfort zone. You have the available time; all you have to do is to start taking baby steps, prioritize, and make a conscious decision you are going after the things important to you.

   It's not difficult to find one hour each day to start working on something you love. All you have to do is use your time wisely. Do you have a long commute? Listen to a podcast in your field of interest. Get up 15 minutes earlier. Shop online to save time or watch less TV.

2. **You have the ability to think and learn:** Most of the things you enjoy today – internet, your car, the house you are living in, etc. are all the results of someone's ability to learn, think, and believe he/she is successful enough to create what you are now enjoying. You have the same abilities to accomplish amazing things with your life, as long as you put your mind to it. While few people in the world are constant thinkers and lifelong learners, you need to do the opposite. Adopt the habit of constantly reading and think of how you can add value to others with the help of your strengths and skills.

3. **You do not need money:** There is a misconception you need money to accomplish most of the things you want in life. You need money to travel, to acquire new experiences, etc. While having money is important for your basic needs, you don't need to be a millionaire to enjoy life. You need to simplify, apply creative thinking, and find ways to do the same thing in a different way. If you want to go on a trip, and you do not have enough money, you do not necessarily have to stay at a hotel, but instead you can stay at a friend's house. If you think you need money for your business, you may want to re-evaluate your business plan to see what you really need, rather than what you think you need. In another scenario, you may try to start a crowdfunding campaign. While you may not have money, there are legitimate ways to find money and support your cause. All you have to do is to think and find a solution as to how you will find what you need.

4. **You have the resources:** Another excuse people use is they do not have the knowledge or contacts, and this is what is stopping them from moving ahead.

You should not be afraid to try to acquire the knowledge you need when you do not have it. No one knows everything anyway, and as technology continually advances, what you knew yesterday may not be valid any more. You should seek to update your knowledge by either taking a class at a college or university, an online course, by using the biggest library that exists – internet, or by finding a mentor and asking him/her to share what he/she knows. No generous person will ever say no to such a request. You can also hire people to do things that are too complicated for you, or you simply do not want to deal with. Always remember you live in a modern society that provides all the modern amenities where you can find all the tools you need to accomplish whatever you want. Imagine how difficult things were 100 years ago or more. Things we now take for granted – as an example, using your car to go to work – were not available. People had to walk to work wasting hours and everything was just a struggle.

CHAPTER 23

INSPIRATIONAL PRINCIPLES AND COMMITMENTS TO LIVE BY

Set up and live your life by the principles and commitments important to you. Your principles can be your source of motivation; they can put you back on track when you are in trouble, and can be a constant reminder as to what is important for you. These are the principles and commitments I made to myself. I understand as life moves forward and I gain new knowledge and experiences, I might adjust some of them. You should create a list of your own principles and stick by them. When you actually see them on paper, it will help you see the big picture, and also understanding who you are and what is valuable to you.

- **Be a bold leader:** This is someone whose thoughts might tell him he is not good enough, but he doesn't listen to them or the people who belittle him and tell him things will not happen; he moves forward regardless. A bold leader is powerful and unstoppable in the face of no agreement.

- **Honor your word:** Make your word count, and always do what you say you will do. If you cannot do what you said you will do, then have a conversation with the person to whom you made the promise and clear that up, as soon as possible.

- **Integrity:** Live life with integrity. As there is no guarantee of the admiration of others, you might as well have integrity. Having integrity will give you the opportunity to be respected.

- **Practice the art of listening:** 1. Ask questions and listen for response. 2. Share yourself. Share aspects of your life important to you, personal or business-related. Make no limit in sharing. 3. Share an embarrassing moment and relate with others.

- **Be unreasonable:** Be unreasonable with yourself and others and make unreasonable requests.

- **Be ten times more excited in life than what you have been:** The purpose of dealing with excitement is to regain your enthusiasm. You can put on, fake, and make up excitement. Commit to memorize and then say something in front of your mirror. Start with four seconds of excitement. Keep on increasing 4 seconds until you can do 2 whole minutes.

- **Be committed, but not attached:** Do everything you can to accomplish your goal, but do not let yourself be attached to the final result. A result at the end, good or bad, is a result. You took action, you tried your best, and at the end that is what matters.

- **Stick with the structure for fulfilment of your goal:** 1. Be emotionally connected with what you want to do. 2. Put yourself at risk. 3. Shoot for the moon. 4. Bring people together and find out how you are going to accomplish your goal.

- **Big goals:** Set big, bold, audacious goals. Often it takes the same effort to accomplish a big goal as it does a much less significant goal. It all comes down to planning and using your resources efficiently.

- **Say "yes" far more than you say "no.":** Try new things, try new ways.

- **Master the art of delegation:** This is a skill many intelligent people struggle with, one that can make a difference between getting things done or not. Having only 24 hours in a day, delegation is the only way to scale up, grow and expand.

- **Control your feelings:** React only to what is important to you. If you allow your feelings to take over, you end up reacting to situations not really important to you. People have power over you, if you react to their situations.

- **Reality:** The way we view life affects our reality. See life from a different positive perspective, and point of view, and your reality will be different.

- **Live without fear and guilt:** Carlos Slim, one of the most successful business people in the world, in a letter to the university community, explained better than anyone else why we should live without fear and guilt. He said, "fear is the worst feeling men can have, it weakens them, inhibits action, and depresses them. Guilt is a tremendous burden in our lives, the way we think and act. Guilt and fear make the present difficult and obstruct the future. To fight them, let us have good sense and accept ourselves as we are, with our realities, our merits, and our sorrows." Fear at the end is a state of mind. Disregard your fears by doing things that scare you. Be fearless in whatever you do, and fear no man.

- **Invalidation:** If people say something that may offend you or invalidate you, don't let it affect you. If you do not let it affect you, then you have complete freedom.

- **Excuses:** Don't let excuses prevent you from doing something.

- **Past/Present/Future:** Live the present intensely and fully, do not let the past be a burden, and let the future be an incentive.

- **See yourself as the ultimate creator:** As a creator, you can create the life you want, exactly the way you want it, and explore an infinite number of possibilities.

- **Be an observer:** Observe what is happening around you and carefully listen. Opportunities may appear when you least expect them.

- **Honesty:** Always be honest with yourself and others.

- **Emotions:** Do not allow negative feelings and emotions to erode your soul. They may pass quickly from your mind, but don't let them stay. Avoid negative emotions such as envy, jealousy, arrogance, lust, selfishness, vengeance, greed, and laziness. Instead, live with positive feelings and emotions such as love, friendship, loyalty, courage, joy, good humor, enthusiasm, peace, serenity, patience, trust, tolerance, prudence, and responsibility.

- **Time:** Time is precious. Don't waste it – make every hour, every moment count.

- **Love:** Love yourself. Love other people. Love nature. Love animals. Love life.

- **Gratitude:** Appreciate everything you ALREADY have in your life. Express gratitude to the people who have touched you. If you do not tell them, they will never know.

- **Respect life:** Life is precious. Respect, value, and protect every type of life.

- **Respect and accept other people as they are:** Respect others for their opinions and who they are. Stop expecting others to behave in a certain way, and don't try to change them. Instead focus on changing yourself. You'll be happier and live a more fulfilling life this way.

- **Obsession:** You need to become so obsessed with your goal; it becomes your ultimate purpose.

- **Kindness:** Be kind to others no matter the circumstances. Start by giving a simple hug, if you feel they need it, or a good positive and encouraging word.

- **Be fair:** Be fair to yourself and other people.

- **Your body:** Nourish your body with healthy food and exercise.

- **Your mind:** Challenge your mind and keep it active.

- **Take risks:** Get out of your comfort zone and take risks often.

- **Experiences:** The goal should be to live life, and have new experiences rather than buy material things. Travel, do things in a different way, meet new people and live the life of your dreams.

- **Regrets:** Do the things you do not want and avoid regrets later in life for not doing them.

- **Deal with things:** Take care of the things that bother you right away rather than wait and keep thinking about them. Deal with them now!

- **Smile/Laugh:** Laugher is one of the best medicines for the soul. Smile and laugh as often as you can.

- **Excellence:** Always seek excellence in everything you do. Excellence is to do the best you can do at that specific moment.

- **Help others:** Help others when you can, for no reason and without expecting something in return. While the intention and the goal should be to help others, do not let people take advantage of you.

- **Help others live their best lives and succeed:** There is no better way to grow than to help others grow and accomplish their goals. Ultimately, the world is one. We are all in this together.

- **Ask for help:** People are eager to help. Don't hesitate to ask for help when you need it.

- **Rejection:** Accept rejection as a learning experience and a necessary step to your path of success.

- **Action:** Take action now – not tomorrow, or later but NOW. Action is a necessary part of success.

- **Procrastination:** When you think you are procrastinating, take action right away.

- **Trust your intuition:** Your instincts and intuition are usually correct. Trust them.

- **Moving forward:** Always move forward, no matter what.

- **Control:** Others have control over you as long as you let them. Always remember in most cases you have control in your life.

- **React:** When you react to other people with negative energy, you give them control over you. React only to what is important for you.

- **Battles:** Pick only the battles worth fighting. Don't waste your time and energy for no reason.

- **Prove:** You don't have to prove anything to anybody. Proving you are right can take a lot of energy for no reason. Let it be.

- **Possibilities:** See possibilities in others, even under the worst circumstances. See possibilities for yourself in everything you do.

- **Thinking:** We are so busy in life we are reacting to everything mechanically. Take the time to think about your life and everything else important to you.

- **Make unreasonable requests:** These are the requests that seem impossible to make under certain circumstances.

- **Be bold:** Take bold actions, and make bold decisions.

- **Defeat:** Don't be afraid to admit defeat and then create new possibilities.

- **Take a stand:** Take a stand for the things, ideas, and people you believe in.

- **Judging:** Don't rush to make quick judgments about people and situations.

- **Beating:** Don't beat yourself when thing go wrong.

- **Inspire:** Inspire yourself and others daily.

- **Accomplishments:** Acknowledge your accomplishments no matter how small you may think they are.

- **Difficult situations:** Confront difficult situations instead of hiding from them.

- **Empathy:** Empathize with others and their situation.

- **Communication:** Offer and ask for open and honest communication.

- **Always seek for happiness:** Let the people, things, and ideas that make you happy inspire and motivate you. Happiness should be the result of your daily existence. Always seek happiness and remember at the end we depart with nothing, we leave behind only our work, family, and friends, and, perhaps, a positive influence which we have planted.

- **Try new things/meet new people:** Seek out new experiences, make new friends, and try to do the same things in a different way.

- **"And", not "Or":** Instead of choosing option A or B, create a third option which includes everything you want.

- **Abundance:** There is unlimited wealth and opportunities for everyone. Focus on getting what you want, rather than worrying if there is enough.

- **Business:** Understand you have only 24 hours in a day and you can't do everything on your own. Scale up by hiring, delegating, outsourcing, or providing your products and services to a large group of people instantaneously. Create passive income streams so your income is not tied to the time you spend on your job.

- **Let go of attachments:** Nothing is permanent in this world, so don't mourn over the loss of something. Be happy it happened instead, and focus on growing and living life to the fullest.

- **Past:** What happened in the past belongs in the past. Don't be held back by what happened yesterday. Live in the present, make a new beginning every day, and plan for the future.

- **Forgiveness:** Forgiveness is healing. Forgive yourself and others often.

- **Criticism:** Accept constructive criticism as something that will help you become better. Rather than reject it, welcome it, celebrate it.

- **Listening:** Pay attention to what other people are saying, and listen for gold, rather than for what may discourage you.

- **Have something at stake:** Having something at stake motivates us to pursue it.

- **Beauty:** Appreciate your beauty, and the beauty of others.

- **Awareness/Live the moment:** When you feel your thoughts wandering around, try to calm your mind down. The forms, colors, sounds, smells we perceive with our senses can only be appreciated when we are aware. Live the moment, be present and aware of what is happening around you. *The only time you're ever living is in this moment, so take full advantage of it.* Meditation and Mindfulness helps being aware and live the moment.

- **Leadership:** Be a leader and create opportunities for yourself and others, and help people live their best life possible.

- **Take the first step:** Don't be afraid to take the first step when others are holding back. Don't wait for others and always take the first step.

- **Decisions:** Follow your intuition and trust your decisions.

- **Be authentic:** You will receive criticism no matter what you do. Be yourself and love yourself for the way you are. Let others see the real you – not the person who you think may like.

- **Enjoy your family and friends:** Spend time with the people in your life who matter the most. Connect with old friends.

- **Build genuine, authentic connections:** Build strong connections with people around you – strangers, friends, family, colleagues, business partners, customers/clients, etc. Spend more time to know them better and foster stronger connections.

- **Responsibility:** You are the only person responsible for your life. If you don't take responsibility for your life, no one will. Stop pushing blame onto others or feel others owe you a living. No one owes you anything, including your family and friends.

- **Results:** The results you get in life are a function of the actions you take. The more actions you take, the more results you will see.

- **Success:** Success in life as a whole is not an external opinion, but rather an internal status. It is the harmony between your soul and your emotions, which requires love, family, friendship, authenticity, and integrity. When you are successful at what you do, it is the result of long periods of hard work that took place long before the point of success.

- **Work:** Don't be afraid to work hard and long hours to get what you want.

- **Unhappiness:** Unhappiness is a product of your thoughts. Make a conscious choice to be happy.

- **Sacrifices:** You have to be eager to make sacrifices and trade time and things you enjoy, to get the things you want and are important to you.

- **Do the right thing:** Do the right thing even though you have to go against everyone else who does not agree with it.

- **Settling:** Don't ever, ever, settle for something less than your ideal. Fight for it. Don't settle for someone you don't really want such as a partner, don't settle for a job you don't like, don't settle for friends who make you feel like a lesser person.

- **Make your own rules:** Play the game, but also make your own rules. Agreements change all the time and what is "the law" today may not exist tomorrow.

- **What's meant to be:** If something is meant to be, it will happen (provided you have already put in the effort). If it hasn't happened yet, it is just not the right time. Be patient and keep doing what you are doing. Your time will come.

- **Do things for yourself:** Don't do things because others asked you to do them. Do it because this is what you want.

- **Above and beyond:** Go above and beyond what is expected from you, and give more value than you receive.

- **Be positive:** Think positive, no matter the circumstances. Positive attitude and thinking will help you accomplish all you want and to live a happy life.

- **Perception:** Everything in life is a matter of perception. Is a glass half full or half empty? Try to see life and things from different angles.

- **Turn complaints into opportunities:** Identify the things you are complaining about and start seeing them as opportunities to learn and grow.

- **Acknowledgement:** Acknowledge others for their accomplishments and their contribution.

- **Compliment:** Genuinely compliment others for their beauty, or anything else that makes them special and unique.

- **Mistakes:** Don't be afraid to make mistakes. Try to make them small, then accept, correct, and forget them. Do not be obsessed by them. Mistakes offer lessons that help us learn and grow and expand.

- **Lead by example:** When you want to inspire others, you need to lead by example. When you preach something and then end up doing something else, not only you do not inspire others, but you lose their respect.

- **Do the things that make you happy:** Your life is too important and your time is too precious to waste them on things that do not make you happy. Be selective and do as much as you can, but only the things you want.

- **What is most valuable in life is free:** Always remember what is most valuable in life does not cost anything but is very precious: love, friendship, nature.

- **Choose happiness:** Happiness IS a Choice!

- **Passion:** Discover your passion in life, ignore the fears stopping you from following it, and make it a full-fledged career. If you have to work for at least 2/3s of your life, you might as well base it on your passion. Aim big. Turn your passion into a huge success and a multi-million dollar business.

- **Live your own life:** Time is limited. Don't waste it living someone else's life through TV characters or celebrities. You need to have your own dreams, goals and inspirations.

- **Opinions:** Don't let the noise of others' opinions drown your inner voice. Make your own decision and trust your intuition.

- **Expectations:** Live by your own expectations and not by other peoples' results or expectations for you. You are unique, you have your own needs and wants, and you should always remember that.

- **Ethics and values:** Live every day by your own set of ethics and values. Be true to them and do not compromise them for any reason.

- **Create your own opportunities:** You can't just sit and wait for opportunities to come into your life. Chances are no one is going to knock on your door with an opportunity. You need to get out there and find ways to create your own.

- **'Softly, softly, catchee monkey'** [1]: When you have a goal you need to understand it may take some time until you achieve it. Be patient, don't get disappointed when obstacles occur; just believe your goal will happen.

- **Believe:** Anything you desire is possible as long as you believe in it. Believe in yourself and your abilities. If you don't, how do you expect others will?

- **Ask:** If you do not ask, you will never get.

- **Possibilities:** There are an infinite number of possibilities for yourself and others. Everything you can imagine is possible as long as you set your heart and soul to it.

- **The squeaky wheel gets the grease:** If you want to get attention, sometimes it is necessary to make a noise or fuss.

- **Motivation:** When you want something badly, with every inch of your existence, then motivation will be there. You don't have to create it or fake it.

- **Life:** Don't wait for life to happen. Chase life. Create life.

- **Pleasing other people:** You can't always please everyone, and if you do, you end up living their life and not yours.

- **People will not always like you:** Some of your decisions may not be acceptable to others. You need to do what feels right for you regardless what others think.

- **Obstacles:** It is a given that while you are going after a goal, obstacles will happen. It is how you deal with them that makes a difference between being successful or not.

- **Stretch your limits:** The only true limit in life is the limits you set for yourself. If you think you can't, then you can't. If instead you think you can, then everything becomes a possibility. Remember the expression "Mind over matter" when you challenge your limits. Stretch your limits, and break them.

- **Mind:** Your mind is the most powerful tool you have. Use it, and challenge it every day.

- **Money:** Money is not everything, but important to do many of the things you want. While many think money is evil, I chose to say I love money and I welcome it in my life.

- **Confidence:** Have confidence in yourself, and remember you are perfect exactly the way you are.

- **Big, audacious goals:** Set big, audacious goals. There are no limits in life – only those you set for yourself.

- **Embrace disappointments:** Disappointments, while

disempowering at the beginning, help us refocus and go stronger after our real goals.

- **Apply the 80/20 Rule:** Spend 20% of effort to get 80% results.

- **Prioritize:** Do the most difficult and important tasks first.

- **Departing:** Everyone has their own beliefs as to what happens when we pass away. I choose to believe there is more – a new spiritual life, after this life ends and our loved ones are just in the next room.

- **Reasons:** Our reasons are not always real. We should choose the reasons that empower us rather than the ones that disempower us.

- **Believe in miracles:** When we believe, miracles happen.

- **Work every day on your goal:** Spend every day working towards your goal even when you do not want to or feel like it.

- **Quitting:** Don't ever quit going after your goals – but, do not be afraid to quit the things that don't serve your purpose.

- **Be proactive:** When you see things going the wrong way, be proactive, and take action to prevent a possible difficult situation.

- **Rest and take breaks often:** When you rest and take breaks when you need to, you reenergize and walk the longer mile ahead.

- **Enjoy the little moments:** There are those little moments that give you the energy to move forward. Soak in the sun on a great day, enjoy nature, enjoy those precious moments with the people you love.

- **Exercise:** Exercise every day – no excuses.

- **Develop your skills to Mastery:** When you do something that seems effortless to others, then it is very possible you have achieved mastery. Commit to getting a huge depth of knowledge – usually it takes 10,000 hours to build mastery in each skill.

- **Seek knowledge:** Learn different skills, pick up different hobbies, study different fields. Be well-rounded with different knowledge, skills, and interests and become a sponge of knowledge and a life-long student.

- **Be well-rounded:** Live the best life possible by having a strong body, mind, excellent relationships with others, and spirituality.

- **Enjoy nature:** Enjoy nature and become one with mother earth.

- **Celebrate your achievements:** Acknowledge and celebrate how far you have come, and all the wonderful things you have accomplished.

- **Separation:** Sometimes separations are difficult, but they are the only way to move forward. If relationships with people don't work for you now, don't be afraid to let them go as something new and more exciting may be ahead.

- **Failure:** Every successful person, one way or another, faced failure towards their path to success. Failure teaches us valuable lessons we can use to our advantage.

- **Cynics, Skeptics, and Pessimists:** Appreciate their point of view, but don't let them influence your way of thinking and your determination to succeed.

- **Don't resist change:** Nothing lasts forever and change will eventually happen. Welcome change, be prepared for change, and if you have good reasons, cause change.

- **If you want to change your life, you need to change life:** All starts with a decision to change things – then you develop a plan as to how you will do it and you follow it step by step.

- **Be open to new ideas:** Be open to new ideas, points of view, and way of doing things. Accept new ideas, even from people you do not agree with since they may have something valuable to say.

- **Focus on your goal:** Spend less time on the things that are not important, focus on your big goal, and do not give up until you accomplish it.

- **Ask often for feedback:** Feedback of friends, family members, colleagues, and mentors can put you on the right track. Ask their feedback often.

- **Have fun:** Remember to set aside time to have fun, let loose, and do the things you really enjoy.

- **You have a choice:** Remember you always have a choice as to how to live your life. If you do not like things the way they are at the moment, make a decision to change, and do what you have to do to change things.

- **Live in alignment with your purpose:** This means anything you do should serve your purpose. If decisions are not aligned with your purpose, you are wasting your time and it will take you longer to get what you want.

- **Decide what you really want:** Life offers so many options. First, you need to decide what you really want. Second, you need to figure out how you will do it. As long as you have your heart and soul in it, you will find the way.

- **Avoid conditional situations:** Conditional situations are when people say they will do X if you do Y. Example, your best friend will love you if you lend him money. These relationships are based on fear and do not last.

- **Comparing:** Don't compare yourself with others. Everyone is different and you are unique in your own way. Everything set in your mind is possible – no one is better (or worse) than you.

- **Be humble:** There is no reason to brag about your accomplishments. Enjoy them and celebrate them with others, but don't make anyone else feel you are better than them.

- **Share your experiences with others:** Don't be afraid to open up and share your experiences, your thoughts and beliefs with others.

- **Competition:** Competing is an opportunity to try your own limits. Do not be afraid to compete and test your limits. As long as the competition is healthy, it is always welcome.

- **Changing people:** You should not try to change people. You need to accept them for who they are.

- **Be generous to others:** Be generous with time, money, and offer valuable advice when needed.

- **Focus on giving rather receiving:** When we do something and we expect something in return, then our motives are not genuine. Not receiving what we expect may lead to disappointment and frustration. When we give without expectations, we are much happier.

- **Focus on what you want, rather than on what you do not have:** Don't spend time thinking of things you do not have. Focus your energy on things you want, use your creativity and your mind to figure out how to get them.

- **Your age:** Be proud of your age, no matter how old you are, and the experiences you have accumulated; you managed to make it so far. Others haven't been so lucky.

- **Do complete work:** Whatever you do, do complete work and what others expect you to do.

- **Put in your maximum effort, even if you don't want to at that moment:** Sometimes it is challenging to do a task when you do not feel like it. This may be because you are tired after a long day at work, or for any other reason. However putting in your maximum effort is needed to get closer to your goal, and feels the most rewarding after you are done.

- **Always move forward:** Remember to always move forward, even if it is at a very slow pace.

- **Control your thoughts:** Controlling your thoughts or not, can be the difference between accomplishing your goals or not. Monitor your thinking and allow only positive thoughts to come in.

- **Make every day an adventure:** Instead of waiting for the weekend to enjoy life, make every day exciting.

- **Life challenges:** Use your life challenges as precious lessons to become stronger.

- **Ideal life:** Create and live your ideal life based on what you want, not what others expect from you.

- **Do something daring every day:** When you do that, you will open yourself to a life full of adventures and exciting possibilities.

- **Principles:** Don't betray your values or principles under any circumstances.

Our principles and commitments can help us find again our inner child and realize what is important to us. Dreams are not impossible when we have an understanding of who we really are, what we really want and what is important to us. Those principles and commitments are fundamental and can act as constant reminders as to where we are at that moment. This is crucial because we can never get a real grasp of where we are going, unless we know where we are now. Our principles and commitments can act as a motivational tool that will inspire action and eventually will help us achieve our dreams and any goal, big or small, we set in our minds.

CHAPTER 24

MOTIVATIONAL QUOTES THAT MOTIVATE FAMOUS PEOPLE

Whan I look for inspiration, I read quotes from famous people to motivate and inspire me to go after my goals and live the extraordinary life I deserve. The value of these quotes is not that they come from "famous" people, but from people like me and you, who in their own way have been there, done that, and managed to overcome their obstacles to become wildly successful. Inspiration though doesn't always come from well-known people. You can get inspiration from anyone who you think is extraordinary in your life, including your friends, family, and colleagues; you appreciate their accomplishments and who they really are. One of my favorite quotes is from my Krav Maga instructor in Toronto, Steven Tierney; "If you train like a cupcake, then you fight like a cupcake".

This is a collection of other favorite quotes [1,2,3,4,5] that motivate me and inspire me every time I read them:

> *"The person who says it cannot be done should not interrupt the person who is doing it."*

> – Chinese Proverb

"The question isn't who is going to let me; it's who is going to stop me."

– Ayn Rand, Russian-American Novelist

"It is never too late to be what you might have been."

– George Eliot, English Novelist, and one of the Leading Writers of the Victorian era

"Do not wait to strike till the iron is hot; but make it hot by striking."

– William B. Sprague, Biographer

"What counts is not necessarily the size of the dog in the fight – it's the size of the fight in the dog."

– Dwight D. Eisenhower, 34th President of the United States

"If you hear a voice within you say, "you cannot paint," then by all means paint and that voice will be silenced."

– Vincent Van Gogh, Post-Impressionist Painter

"If not you, then who? If not now, when?"

– Hillel the Elder, Jewish Religious Leader

"Your time is limited, so don't waste it living someone else's life. Don't be trapped by dogma – which is living with the results of other people's thinking. Don't let the noise of others' opinions drown out your own inner voice. And most important, have the courage to follow your heart and intuition."

– Steve Jobs, Cofounder of Apple Inc.

"Be kind, for everyone you meet is fighting a hard battle."

– Socrates, Greek Philosopher

"Nothing is impossible, the word itself says, "I'm possible!"

– Audrey Hepburn, British Actress and Humanitarian

"Our premise is and has always been that we leave with nothing; that we can only do things while we are alive and that businessmen are creators of the wealth they temporarily manage."

– Carlos Slim, Mexican Business Magnate

"Nothing is particularly hard if you divide it into smaller parts."

– Henry Ford, American Industrialist, Founder of the Ford Motor Company

"Man sacrifices his health in order to make money. Then he sacrifices money to recuperate his health. And then he is so anxious about the future that he does not enjoy the present; the result being that he does not live in the present or the future; he lives as if he is never to die, and then dies having never really lived."

– Dalai Lama

"The price of anything is the amount of life you exchange for it."

– Henry David Thoreau, American Author, Poet, Philosopher

"It does not matter how slowly you go as long as you do not stop."

– Confucius, Chinese Teacher, Editor, Politician, and Philosopher

"There is only one way to avoid criticism: do nothing, say nothing, and be nothing."

– Aristotle, Greek Philosopher

"Ask and it will be given to you; search, and you will find; knock and the door will be opened for you."

– Jesus

"Challenge yourself with something you know you could never do, and what you'll find is that you can overcome anything."

– Anonymous

"Human behavior flows from three main sources: desire, emotion, and knowledge."

– Plato, Philosopher, Mathematician

"The more things you do, the more you can do."

– Lucille Ball, American Actress, Comedian

"The will to win, the desire to succeed, the urge to reach your full potential... these are the keys that will unlock the door to personal excellence."

– Confucius, Chinese Teacher, Editor, Politician, Philosopher

"Logic will get you from A to B. Imagination will take you everywhere."

– Albert Einstein, Theoretical Physicist

"Intelligence is the ability to adapt to change"

– Stephen Hawking, Theoretical Physicist

"Don't let mental blocks control you. Set yourself free. Confront your fear and turn the mental blocks into building blocks."

– Roopleen, Author

"We need to understand that Ideas have more power than the physical brains that give birth to them. Ideas have the power to live on, after the brain that creates them has returned to dust. Examples are philosophies and ideas from people who have passed on, yet their ideas are still alive. We need to give

time to the ideas to mature and grow to their full potential."

– Napoleon Hill, Personal Success Author

"Don't wait for the end of the weekend to have fun, or Sunday to rest. Live and take action today"

– Odysseas Elytis, Greek Poet, Nobel Prize in Literature

"If you don't value your time, neither will others. Stop giving away your time and talents. Value what you know & start charging for it."

– Kim Garst, Founder and CEO of Boom!

"Live as if you were to die tomorrow. Learn as if you were to live forever."

– Mahatma Gandhi, Leader of Indian Independence Movement

"If you genuinely want something, don't wait for it – teach yourself to be impatient."

– Gurbaksh Chahal, Internet Entrepreneur and Writer

"Don't let the fear of losing be greater than the excitement of winning."

– Robert Kiyosaki, American Investor, Businessman, Self-Help Author

"If you want to make a permanent change, stop focusing on the size of your problems and start focusing on the size of you!"

– T. Harv Eker, Author, Businessman and Motivational Speaker

"You can't connect the dots looking forward; you can only connect them looking backwards. So you have to trust that the dots will somehow connect in your future. You have to trust in something – your gut, destiny, life, karma, whatever. This approach has never let me down, and it has made all the difference in my life."

– Steve Jobs, Cofounder of Apple Inc.

"Each morning when I open my eyes I say to myself: I, not events, have the power to make me happy or unhappy today. I can choose which it shall be. Yesterday is dead, tomorrow hasn't arrived yet. I have just one day, today, and I'm going to be happy in it."

– Groucho Marx, American Comedian, Film and Television Star

"Welcome every morning with a smile. Look on the new day as another special gift from your Creator, another golden opportunity to complete what you were unable to finish yesterday. Be a self-starter. Let your first hour set the theme of success and positive action that is certain to echo through your entire day. Today will never happen again. Don't waste it with a false start or no start at all. You were not born to fail."

– Og Mandino, American Author

"Optimism is the most important human trait, because it allows us to evolve our ideas, to improve our situation, and to hope for a better tomorrow."

– Seth Godin, American Author

"Each problem has hidden in it an opportunity so powerful that it literally dwarfs the problem. The greatest success stories were created by people who recognized a problem and turned it into an opportunity."

– Joseph Sugarman, Author

"We can't escape pain; we can't escape the essential nature of our lives. But we do have a choice. We can give in and relent, or we can fight, persevere, and create a life worth living, a noble life. Pain is a fact; our evaluation of it is a choice."

– Jacob Held, Associate Professor and Director of UCA Core

"Write it on your heart that every day is the best day in the year."

– Ralph Waldo Emerson, American Essayist, Lecturer, and Poet

"You cannot tailor-make the situations in life but you can tailor-make the attitudes to fit those situations."

– Zig Ziglar, American Author and Motivational Speaker

"Winners lose much more often than losers. So if you keep losing, but you're still trying, keep it up! You're right on track."

– Matthew Keith Groves, Poet

"Motivation is a fire from within. If someone else tries to light that fire under you, chances are it will burn very briefly."

– Stephen R. Covey, Author, Educator, Keynote Speaker

"Positive anything is better than negative thinking."

– Elbert Hubbard, American Writer, Publisher, Artist, and Philosopher

"If you don't go after what you want, you'll never have it. If you don't ask, the answer is always no. If you don't step forward, you're always in the same place."

– Nora Roberts, American Bestselling Author

"Begin with the end in mind."

– Stephen R. Covey, Author, Educator, Keynote Speaker

"Too many of us are not living our dreams because we are living our fears."

– Les Brown, Motivational Speaker

"Whether you think you can or think you can't, you're right."

– Henry Ford, American Industrialist

"The difference between a successful person and others is not lack of strength not a lack of knowledge but rather a lack of will."

– Vince Lombardi, American Football Player

"Success seems to be connected with action. Successful people keep moving. They make mistakes but don't quit."

– Conrad Hilton, American Hotelier

"Either you run the day, or the day runs you."

– Jim Rohn, American Entrepreneur, Author and Motivational Speaker

"The surest way not to fail is to determine to succeed."

– Richard B. Sheridan, Irish Playwright and Poet

"Desire is the starting point of all achievement, not a hope, not a wish, but a keen pulsating desire, which transcends everything."

– Napoleon Hill, Personal Success Author

"Great spirits have always encountered violent opposition from mediocre minds".

– Albert Einstein, Theoretical Physicist

*"In every difficult situation is potential value. Believe this,
then begin looking for it."*

– Norman Vincent Peale, Minister, Author and a Progenitor of
"positive thinking"

"Nothing great was ever achieved without enthusiasm."

– Ralph Waldo Emerson, American Essayist, Lecturer, and Poet

*"Knowing is not enough; we must apply. Willing is not
enough; we must do."*

– Johann Wolfgang von Goethe, German Writer and Statesman

*"We are what we repeatedly do. Excellence, therefore, is not an
act but a habit."*

– Aristotle, Greek Philosopher

*"When you get into a tight place and everything goes against
you, till it seems you could not hang on a minute longer, never
give up then, for that is just the place and time that the tide
will turn."*

– Harriet Beecher Stowe, American Abolitionist and Author

"Well begun is half done"

– Greek Proverb

"Life consists not in holding good cards, but in playing those you hold well."

– Josh Billings, American Humorist

"He who hesitates is lost."

– Proverb

"If you want to succeed in the world you must make your own opportunities as you go on. The man who waits for some seventh wave to toss him on dry land will find that the seventh wave is a long time a coming. You can commit no greater folly than to sit by the roadside until someone comes along and invites you to ride with him to wealth or influence."

– John B. Gough, United States Temperance Orator

"All our dreams can come true, if we have the courage to pursue them."

– Walt Disney, American Business Magnate, Cartoonist, Animator, Film Producer

"If opportunity doesn't knock, build a door."

– Milton Berle, American Comedian and Actor

"Many of life's failures are experienced by people who did not realize how close they were to success when they gave up."

– Thomas Edison, American Inventor and Businessman

"I am always doing that which I cannot do, in order that I may learn how to do it."

– Pablo Picasso, Spanish Painter

"I haven't failed. I've just found 10,000 ways that won't work."

– Thomas Edison, American Inventor and Businessman

"People who are crazy enough to think they can change the world, are the ones who do."

– Rob Siltanen, Chairman and Chief Creative Officer at Siltanen & Partners

"The pessimist sees difficulty in every opportunity. The optimist sees the opportunity in every difficulty."

– Winston Churchill, British Politician

"You see things; and you say "Why?" But I dream things that never were; and I say "Why not?"

– George Bernard Shaw, Irish Playwright

"A successful man is one who can lay a firm foundation with the bricks that others throw at him."

– Sidney Greenberg, American Author

"It is the mark of an educated mind to be able to entertain a thought without accepting it."

– Aristotle, Greek Philosopher

"Great minds discuss ideas; average minds discuss events; small minds discuss people."

– Eleanor Roosevelt, American Politician

"In any situation, the best thing you can do is the right thing; the next best thing you can do is the wrong thing; the worst thing you can do is nothing."

– Theodore Roosevelt, American Politician

"Fearlessness is the mother of reinvention."

– Arianna Huffington, Greek-American Author and Syndicated Columnist

"I am the wisest man alive, for I know one thing, and that is that I know nothing."

– Socrates, Greek Philosopher

"Employ your time in improving yourself by other men's writings, so that you shall gain easily what others have labored hard for."

– Socrates, Greek Philosopher

"I am not an Athenian or a Greek; I am a citizen of the world."

– Socrates, Greek Philosopher

"Success is about creating benefit for all and enjoying the process. If you focus on this & adopt this definition, success is yours."

– Kelly Kim, Poker Player

"You have to learn the rules of the game. And then you have to play better than anyone else."

– Albert Einstein, Theoretical Physicist

"Every great dream begins with a dreamer. Always remember, you have within you the strength, the patience, and the passion to reach for the stars to change the world."

– Harriet Tubman, African-American Abolitionist, Humanitarian

"The successful warrior is the average man, with laser-like focus."

– Bruce Lee, Martial Artist

"Very often a change of self is needed more than a change of scene."

– Arthur Christopher Benson, English Essayist, Poet, and Author

"In doubtful matters boldness is everything."

– Publilius Syrus, Latin Writer of Sententiae

"Never let your memories be greater than your dreams."

– Doug Ivester, Chairman and Chief Executive Officer of Coca-Cola Company

"Success is going from failure to failure without losing your enthusiasm."

– Winston Churchill, British Politician

"The journey of a thousand miles begins with one step."

– Lao Tzu, Philosopher and Poet of Ancient China

"Action is the foundational key to all success"

– Pablo Picasso, Spanish Painter

"The creation of a thousand forests is in one acorn."

– Ralph Waldo Emerson, American Essayist, Lecturer, and Poet

"It's not whether you get knocked down; it's whether you get up."

– Vince Lombardi, American Football Player

"What the mind of man can conceive and believe, it can achieve."

– Napoleon Hill, Personal Success Author

"It wasn't raining when Noah built the ark."

– Howard Ruff, Financial Adviser and Writer

"Dream big and dare to fail."

– Norman Vaughan, English Comedian

"What you do speaks so loudly that I cannot hear what you say."

– Ralph Waldo Emerson, American Essayist, Lecturer, and Poet

"You must be the change you wish to see in the world."

– Gandhi, Preeminent Leader of Indian Independence Movement

"Tough times never last, but tough people do."

– Dr. Robert Schuller, American Televangelist, Pastor, Motivational
Speaker

*"There is only one success: to be able to spend your life in your
own way."*

– Christopher Morley, American Journalist, Novelist, Essayist and
Poet

"The power of imagination makes us infinite."

– John Muir. Scottish-American Naturalist, Author

"The best dreams happen when you're awake."

– Cherie Gilderbloom

"Believe and act as if it were impossible to fail."

– Charles Kettering, American Inventor, Engineer, Businessman

"Don't count the days, make the days count."

– Muhammad Ali, Professional Boxer

"The difference between ordinary and extraordinary is that little extra."

– Jimmy Johnson, American Football Broadcaster

"Believe you can and you're halfway there."

– Theodore Roosevelt, American Politician

"Don't wait. The time will never be just right."

– Napoleon Hill, Personal Success Author

"Everything you've ever wanted is on the other side of fear."

– George Addair, Real-Estate Developer in Post-Civil War Atlanta

"A year from now you may wish you had started today."

– Karen Lamb, Author

"There are no traffic jams along the extra mile."

– Roger Staubach, National Football League Quarterback

"Do what you can, where you are, with what you have."

– Teddy Roosevelt , American Politician

"What we fear doing most is usually what we most need to do."

– Tim Ferriss, American Author, Entrepreneur, Angel Investor, and Public Speaker

"To avoid criticism, do nothing, say nothing, be nothing."

– Elbert Hubbard, American Writer, Publisher, Artist, and Philosopher

"Your imagination is your preview of life's coming attractions."

– Albert Einstein, Theoretical Physicist

"The purpose of our lives is to be happy."

– Dalai Lama

"The best way to predict the future is to invent it."

– Alan Kay, American Computer Scientist

"If you have everything under control, you're not moving fast enough."

– Mario Andretti, Retired Italian American World Champion Racing Driver

"Remember that not getting what you want is sometimes a wonderful stroke of luck."

– Dalai Lama

"A champion is someone who gets up, even when he can't."

– Unknown

"If you do what you've always done, you'll get what you've always gotten."

– Tony Robbins, American Life Coach and Self-Help Author

"It's not the years in your life that count. It's the life in your years."

– Abraham Lincoln, 16th President of the United States

"Change your thoughts and you change your world."

– Norman Vincent Peale, Minister, Author and a Progenitor of "positive thinking"

"Either write something worth reading or do something worth writing."

– Benjamin Franklin, one of the Founding Fathers of the United States

"When everything seems to be going against you, remember that the airplane takes off against the wind, not with it."

– Henry Ford, American Industrialist

"Control Your Own Destiny or Someone Else Will"

– Jack Welch, Retired American Business Executive, Author and Chemical Engineer

"Motivation gets you going and habit gets you there."

– Zig Ziglar, American Author and Motivational Speaker

"People often say that motivation doesn't last. Well, neither does bathing - that's why we recommend it daily."

– Zig Ziglar, American Author and Motivational Speaker

"Do you want to know who you are? Don't ask. Act! Action will delineate and define you."

– Thomas Jefferson, American Founding Father

"The way to get started is to quit talking and begin doing "

– Walt Disney Company

"Get going. Move forward. Aim High. Plan a takeoff. Don't just sit on the runway and hope someone will come along and push the airplane. It simply won't happen. Change your attitude and gain some altitude. Believe me, you'll love it up here."

– Donald Trump, American Businessman

"Don't watch the clock; do what it does. Keep going."

– Sam Levenson, American Humorist, Writer, Teacher, Television Host, and Journalist

"You miss 100% of the shots you don't take."

– Wayne Gretzky, Canadian Former Professional Ice Hockey Player

"Whatever the mind of man can conceive and believe, it can achieve."

– Napoleon Hill, Personal Success Author

"I've missed more than 9000 shots in my career. I've lost almost 300 games. 26 times I've been trusted to take the game winning shot and missed. I've failed over and over and over again in my life. And that is why I succeed."

– Michael Jordan, Professional Basketball Player

"Twenty years from now you will be more disappointed by the things that you didn't do than by the ones you did do, so throw off the bowlines, sail away from safe harbor, catch the trade winds in your sails. Explore, Dream, Discover."

– Mark Twain, American Author and Humorist

315

"An unexamined life is not worth living."

– Socrates, Greek Philosopher

"Whatever you can do, or dream you can, begin it. Boldness has genius, power and magic in it."

– Johann Wolfgang von Goethe, German Writer and Statesman

"We can easily forgive a child who is afraid of the dark; the real tragedy of life is when men are afraid of the light."

– Plato, Greek Philosopher, and Mathematician

"Start where you are. Use what you have. Do what you can."

– Arthur Ashe, American World No. 1 Professional Tennis Player

"You give before you get."

– Napoleon Hill, Personal Success Author

"When I was 5 years old, my mother always told me that happiness was the key to life. When I went to school, they

asked me what I wanted to be when I grew up. I wrote down 'happy'. They told me I didn't understand the assignment, and I told them they didn't understand life."

– John Lennon, English Musician, Singer and Songwriter

"When one door of happiness closes, another opens, but often we look so long at the closed door that we do not see the one that has been opened for us."

– Helen Keller, American Author, Political Activist, and Lecturer

"Everything has beauty, but not everyone can see."

– Confucius, Chinese Teacher, Editor, Politician, and Philosopher

"First, have a definite, clear practical ideal; a goal, an objective. Second, have the necessary means to achieve your ends; wisdom, money, materials, and methods. Third, adjust all your means to that end."

– Aristotle, Greek Philosopher and Scientist

"Too many of us are not living our dreams because we are living our fears."

– Les Brown, Motivational Speaker

317

"Whatever your mind can conceive and can believe, it can achieve."

– Napoleon Hill, Personal Success Author

"I have been impressed with the urgency of doing. Knowing is not enough; we must apply. Being willing is not enough; we must do."

– Leonardo da Vinci, Italian Polymath, Painter, Sculptor, Architect, Inventor,

"Limitations live only in our minds. But if we use our imaginations, our possibilities become limitless."

– Jamie Paolinetti, American Cyclist

"What's money? A man is a success if he gets up in the morning and goes to bed at night and in between does what he wants to do."

– Bob Dylan, American Singer-Songwriter, Artist and Writer

"Build your own dreams, or someone else will hire you to build theirs."

– Farrah Gray, American Businessman, Investor, Philanthropist

"The battles that count aren't the ones for gold medals. The struggles within yourself–the invisible battles inside all of us– that's where it's at."

– Jesse Owens, Four-Time Olympic Gold Medalist

"Strength does not come from physical capacity. It comes from an indomitable will."

– Mahatma Gandhi, Preeminent Leader of Indian Independence Movement

"Do not go where the path may lead, go instead where there is no path and leave a trail."

– Waldo Emerson, American Essayist, Lecturer, and Poet

"Whatever we think about and thank about we bring about."

– John Demartini, Best Selling Author

"Whether you think you can or can't either way you are right."

– Henry Ford, American Industrialist

"The vast majority of people are born, grow up, struggle and go through life in misery and failure, not realizing that it would be just as easy to switch over and get exactly what they want out of life, not recognizing that the mind attracts the thing it dwells upon."

– Napoleon Hill, Personal Success Author

While this list of quotes is very inspiring, don't be afraid to be the creator; develop your own quotes that make sense to you and you want to live your life by. While similar, everyone is different, everyone has different needs and everyone has their potential to inspire with their own words themselves and others. Who are you really? What knowledge and beliefs do you have that you would like to share? What words can you write that will inspire you and motivate you? Become the creator and change to the better your life and the life of others.

These are two of my own quotes that inspire me and motivate me:

"By becoming a writer I realized that I will live forever."

– Manos Filippou, Author

"The sky is not the limit. You are your limits. Break them today!"

– Manos Filippou, Author

320

CHAPTER 25

ABOUT THE AUTHOR

At a younger age, I used to believe that in life we can only be one thing, and this is what defines us. The society, my environment, and the messages I was getting, taught me to see myself and other people only through one filter rather through multiple filters that actually show who we really are. Names based on a career choice, or personal characteristics, such as "John, the dentist", "Elisa, the pretty girl", etc. are a good example of the one-dimensional messages I was getting which contributed to subconsciously putting limitations on myself.

The reality though is we are not defined by only one thing, and in our own way, we all have many dimensions. You can get a better understanding of this by taking the time to think about all the different lives you live, and you have lived. You have a family life, a work life, a life with your friends and so many other lives based on the communities and interests you are involved in. Each community may know a different side of you. Your family may know you as a caring mother, father, son, or daughter, while at work you may be known as the strict boss, or at your gym club you may be known as a highly-skilled athlete. Your dominant characteristic at a specific community, maybe define how you are viewed.

We are, can be, and can do many things at the same time; we can be highly successful in each key field of our life. We must not put limitations on ourselves as to who we think we are, and what we can do. What we do at the present moment does not define our possibilities and our success levels in the future.

When I realized I do not have any limitations, I decided to learn many new skills and explore many passions, and do many of the things I always wanted to do. While at the moment my focus is writing, through coaching, motivating, and helping people reach their full potential, there are many other passions and things personal or professional, I have explored and enjoy doing.

Top Interesting Facts About Me

- I am a successful Marketing Expert for Family Lawyers for over 4 years.

- I have over 15 years' experience as an Internet Marketing Consultant, Website Developer, and Graphic Designer.

- I am a serial entrepreneur, exploring various business ventures. At the moment I have an aerial photography & cinematography business and love flying drones.

- I am a Certified Chair Massage Practitioner.

- I have been involved in philanthropic projects; In 2013 I founded "Project Hermes", an internet marketing program, training unemployed young Greeks.

- I have a University Degree in Business Administration.

- I have successfully completed the Landmark Education,

Self-Expression and Leadership Program and have taken many other self-development courses.

- I served for a year with the Greek Army and was trained as a Topographer.

- I love martial arts and have a yellow belt in Krav Maga, the defense system of the Israeli Defense Force.

- I grew up in Greece, and live in Canada. I love traveling and have visited over a dozen countries, many of them multiple times.

- I have self-taught myself many new skills. I love educating myself by reading or taking online courses.

- I take care of my body and keeping fit is a top priority.

- I enjoy challenging my mind and playing board games, especially scrabble.

As my goals and needs evolve, I'm looking forward to gaining new knowledge, living new experiences, meeting new exciting people, and building new memories. Welcome to my world and life.

CHAPTER 26

FINAL WORDS – MISSION

My mission is to help people reach their full potential, whatever that might be, and touch, move, and inspire others by following ethical standards, being dedicated to their needs, and committed to excellence. I do this by sharing knowledge, listening when there is an opportunity, motivating, and encouraging.

Touching, moving, and inspiring: I want to touch, move, inspire, and motivate people to go after what they really want in life. I see people having astonishing possibilities, which many times they don't even realize and all they need is a little push to move forward. It is really an amazing feeling helping people reach their full potential and by helping others to be successful, I also have the opportunity to reach, fine-tune, and optimize my own greatness.

Sharing knowledge: Sharing knowledge and experiences is crucial when trying to help others. The goal is to help people understand and relate. We are all in this together. We just have different goals and points of view. Two people may do exactly the same thing, but they may see things from a totally different perspective. This is why sharing is important because it may give us the chance to discover something we never considered before.

Listening: As an observer, I listen without making any judgments about what people have to say; I motivate them to accomplish what they are really after, and help them make a difference in their lives and what is important to them. Of course, when asked, I provide an honest and direct point of view.

Motivating: My commitment is to motivate people to create experiences for themselves and others – no matter their age, sex, financial status, religion, or stage of life they are in. The ultimate goal is to help them achieve happiness with what they are doing, and live the best life possible.

Encouraging: We are all in this and everyone deserves to have a great life – even the people we do not like, or we do not agree with. My commitment is to make a significant impact, and encourage and support people to change their lives, and the lives of others for the better and have long-lasting results. Sometimes, this happens slowly and step-by-step, but it eventually happens. Changing habits and starting to see what is possible, to eliminate fear, and to make the decision to take action – continuously, to find a life's purpose and ultimately what makes us happy, are not things that happen instantly after all.

If this book helps you start thinking about new possibilities, or you learned something new, or you realized something you were not aware, or helped you see things from a different perspective, then I'm accomplishing my goal. And, if it refreshes what you may have heard or learned before, well, that too is great.

My mission though doesn't end here. My intention is to meet people in person through private group classes, business and social events, or through one-to-one motivational coaching. I'm looking forward to inspiring others and also being inspired by the human determination, spirit, and possibilities.

EPILOGUE

You have the power, you have the strength, you are amazing, and you can accomplish anything you set your mind to. The sky is not the limit, you are your limits. Break them today by doing something you love and going after the things you really want. Be ethical and have integrity, follow the rules, yet educate yourself, expand and set up your own rules. If I can do it, then I'm sure you can. Avoid mediocrity and reach for your full potential, whatever that may be. Dig deep inside your soul and find again your inner child. What does the younger version of you really want? Ask him/her and you will get all the answers.

You have only one life to live and every day is precious. It is your obligation to reach your full potential and leave your own mark on this planet. People may not always tell you, because they do not always have the courage, or they do not know how to express themselves, but you DO matter, and you are loved and appreciated for who you are. Stop listening to the ones who hold you back and your negative thoughts that tell you, "You can't". You can absolutely do anything and can be anything you want, no matter your age, your sex, your race, your religion and your ethnicity. Next time you have your doubts, and you think "I give up, I prefer to just stay in my comfort zone and watch TV", look at the "stupid box" as many people call it and realize what you have in front of you. This box was invented by a 14-year-old farm boy, where in 1922 he first sketched his idea for television for his science teacher [1]. The boy's name was Philo T. Farnsworth and he knew very little about electronic theory. Today almost everyone has a TV in their house and they can see live images from the other side of the planet. Think about it. It is absolutely amazing and just less than 100 years ago most of us would have thought – it's impossible for such a device to exist. Look around you at the basic things you use and enjoy every day and take for granted. Your phone, your car, internet; all these things are products of someone's imagination, their belief they could do it, and their determination to make those things happen.

You have the potential to accomplish absolutely anything you want in your life, as long as you put your mind to it. I know a lot of people reading this book will find it a source of motivation and a valuable tool that will help them take action. For the people who still have doubt and they think they can't, I will conclude this book by asking two simple questions. Have you tried with every inch of your being and do you know FOR SURE you can't? And what is the ACTUAL COST to you and to the people who love you for not getting out of your comfort zone and reaching your full potential?

ACKNOWLEDGEMENTS AND BIBLIOGRAPHY

"It is never too late to be what you might have been."[1]

– George Eliot, English Novelist and one of the Leading Writers of the Victorian era

Napoleon Hill, Think and Grow Rich, 1937 (Public Domain)
3. Bob Proctor, The Science Of Getting Rich Video Training
www.youtube.com/watch?v=AEWJxYzikAo

3   Our Belief System And Paradigms   21

1. www.brainyquote.com/quotes/quotes/t/tonyrobbin147773.html
2. http://mobilecityservices.com/category/lifestyle/
3. http://advancedlifeskills.com/blog/how-your-beliefs-create-your-reality-part-2/
4. http://advancedlifeskills.com/blog/how-your-beliefs-create-your-reality-part-2/
5. www.brainyquote.com/quotes/quotes/m/muhammadal120238.html?src=t_belief
6. http://annrusnak.com/mind-power-secrets-the-law-of-repetition/
7. http://annrusnak.com/mind-power-secrets-the-law-of-repetition/
8. http://beliefdoctor.com/faq/what-is-a-belief-system
9. Bob Proctor, The Science Of Getting Rich Video Training
www.youtube.com/watch?v=AEWJxYzikAo
10. Napoleon Hill, Think and Grow Rich, 1937 (Public Domain)
11. http://advancedlifeskills.com/blog/how-your-beliefs-create-your-reality-part-1/
12. http://advancedlifeskills.com/blog/how-your-beliefs-create-your-reality-part-2/
13. http://advancedlifeskills.com/blog/how-your-beliefs-create-your-reality-part-3/

14. http://advancedlifeskills.com/blog/how-your-beliefs-create-your-reality-part-4/
15. http://advancedlifeskills.com/blog/how-your-beliefs-create-your-reality-part-5/
16. http://mobilecityservices.com/timetip-2-single-thing-controls-95-life/

4   Creative Process   33

1. www.brainyquote.com/citation/quotes/quotes/c/confucius119275.html#d0BtseZutQixrToh.99
2. Vera Nazarian, The Perpetual Calendar of Inspiration www.goodreads.com/quotes/512326-one-of-the-strangest-things-is-the-act-of-creation
3. www.tom2tall.com/Napoleon-Hill-Quotes.html www.goodreads.com/work/quotes/14364793-the-perpetual-calendar-of-inspiration
4. www.nightingale.com/articles/napoleon-hills-think-and-grow-rich/
5. http://brightdrops.com/best-motivational-quotes
6. www.brainyquote.com/quotes/quotes/c/confucius140908.html?src=t_motivational
7. Bob Proctor, The Science Of Getting Rich Video Training www.youtube.com/watch?v=AEWJxYzikAo
8. Bob Proctor, The Science Of Getting Rich Video Training www.youtube.com/watch?v=AEWJxYzikAo
9. http://genius.com/Napoleon-hill-think-and-grow-rich-chapter-9-annotated
10. www.brainyquote.com/quotes/quotes/s/swami-vivek213397.html
11. www.brainyquote.com/quotes/quotes/n/napoleon-hi393412.html

12. http://genius.com/Napoleon-hill-think-and-grow-rich-chapter-6-annotated
13. https://books.google.ca/books?isbn=1604500077
14. Bob Proctor, The Science Of Getting Rich Video Training www.youtube.com/watch?v=AEWJxYzikAo
15. Napoleon Hill, Think and Grow Rich, 1937 (Public Domain)

5 Make The Decision   45

1. www.brainyquote.com/quotes/authors/n/noreena_hertz.html
2. www.brainyquote.com/quotes/authors/g/gretchen_rubin.html
   https://gretchenrubin.com/happiness_project/2014/02/the-habits-we-most-want-to-foster-or-the-essential-seven/
3. http://brightdrops.com/best-motivational-quotes
4. Steve Jobs. BrainyQuote.com, Xplore Inc, 2015. www.brainyquote.com/quotes/quotes/s/stevejobs416854.html.
5. Napoleon Hill, Think and Grow Rich, 1937 (Public Domain)

6 Set Clear Goals   53

1. www.brainyquote.com/quotes/quotes/b/brian-tracy173268.html
2. http://brightdrops.com/best-motivational-quotes
3. www.wikihow.com/Set-Goals
4. www.wikihow.com/Set-SMART-Goals

5. http://ajwalton.com/famous-success-quotes-inspire-greatness/

7   Think Positive   61

1. https://books.google.ca/books?id=5K7DAgAAQBAJ&pg=PA135&lpg=PA135&dq=Who+told+you+it+couldn%27t+be+done?+And+what+great+achievement+has+he+to+his+credit+that+entitles+him-+to+use+the+word+%27impossible%27+so+freely&source=bl&ots=DaOaFAAfiz&sig=4FxN70N-zQD-vR-Ro5HntWr43800&hl=en&sa=X&ei=iweS-Vb2eLMzf-QGiwbnwCQ&ved=0CB0Q6AEwAA#v=onepage&q=Who%20told%20you%20it%20couldn't%20be%20done%3F%20And%20what%20great%20achievement%20has%20he%20to%20his%20credit%20that%20entitles%20him%20to%20use%20the%20word%20'impossible'%20so%20freely&f=false
2. www.wikihow.com/Think-Positively
3. http://advancedlifeskills.com/blog/how-do-appreciation-and-gratitude-affect-your-life/
4. www.wikihow.com/Think-Positively
5. www.azquotes.com/quote/780276
6. http://advancedlifeskills.com/blog/how-do-appreciation-and-gratitude-affect-your-life/
7. Napoleon Hill, Think and Grow Rich, 1937 (Public Domain)
8. www.wikihow.com/Be-More-Mentally-Aware
9. www.psychologytoday.com/blog/pathological-relationships/201206/becoming-aware
10. http://kerrybrook.ca/resources_articles_books_counselling/tools_for_the_aware_self_to_use

11. www.thebestbrainpossible.com/the-meaning-of-mind-fulness-2/

12. www.oxforddictionaries.com/definition/english/mind-fulness

8 Awareness   73

1. www.psychologytoday.com/blog/pathological-relation-ships/201206/becoming-aware

2. Bob Proctor, The Science Of Getting Rich Video Training
www.youtube.com/watch?v=AEWJxYzikAo

3. Bob Proctor, The Science Of Getting Rich Video Training
www.youtube.com/watch?v=AEWJxYzikAo

4. www.wikihow.com/Be-More-Mentally-Aware

5. www.psychologytoday.com/basics/stress

6. www.psychologytoday.com/blog/pathological-relation-ships/201206/becoming-aware

7. www.wikihow.com/Think-Positively

8. http://kerrybrook.ca/resources_articles_books_counsel-ling/tools_for_the_aware_self_to_use

9. Jon Kabat-Zinn www.mindfulnesscds.com/

9 Believe   81

1. www.values.com/inspirational-quotes/3204-you-have-to-believe-in-yourself-thats-the

2. www.goodreads.com/quotes/32753-man-often-becomes-what-he-believes-himself-to-be-if

3. www.robsmithcounsel.com/whatever-the-mind-can-conceive-the-mind-can-achieve/

4. www.excelatlife.com/articles/generalizing.htm

5. Napoleon Hill, Think and Grow Rich, 1937 (Public Domain)
6. www.mariaevesonline.com/think-and-grow-rich-chapter-4-autosuggestion/
7. Napoleon Hill, Think and Grow Rich, 1937 (Public Domain)
8. www.wikihow.com/Use-Autosuggestion
9. www.wikihow.com/Build-Self-Confidence
10. www.wikihow.com/Sample/Ways-to-Build-Confidence

10 Willpower   91

1. www.brainyquote.com/quotes/quotes/d/danmillman173284.html
2. www.goodreads.com/quotes/104137-the-man-who-goes-farthest-is-generally-the-one-who
3. www.brainyquote.com/quotes/quotes/a/aleistercr386874.html
4. www.azquotes.com/quote/831693
5. www.goodreads.com/quotes/593367-the-will-is-the-keystone-in-the-arch-of-human
6. www.notable-quotes.com/w/willpower_quotes.html
7. www.brainyquote.com/quotes/quotes/c/confucius119275.html
8. www.lifehack.org/articles/communication/15-ways-increase-our-willpower.html
9. www.entrepreneur.com/article/230378
10. www.earlytorise.com/one-factor-that-changes-everything/
11. www.lifehack.org/articles/communication/15-ways-increase-our-willpower.html

12. www.psychologytoday.com/blog/good-thinking/201306/how-boost-your-willpower
13. www.thefeelgoodlifestyle.com/willpower-discipline.html
14. www.thefeelgoodlifestyle.com/willpower-discipline.html
15. www.thefeelgoodlifestyle.com/willpower-discipline.html
16. http://operationmeditation.com/discover/8-strategic-steps-on-how-to-increase-will-power/
17. www.artofmanliness.com/2012/01/15/how-to-strengthen-willpower/
18. www.artofmanliness.com/2012/01/15/how-to-strengthen-willpower/
19. www.artofmanliness.com/2012/01/15/how-to-strengthen-willpower/
20. www.thefeelgoodlifestyle.com/willpower-discipline.html
21. https://blog.bufferapp.com/dont-stop-procrastinating-procrastination-doesnt-need-a-cure-structured-distraction
22. www.entrepreneur.com/article/226017
23. www.earlytorise.com/one-factor-that-changes-everything/
24. http://sidsavara.com/personal-development/will-power-how-to-improve-your-personal-self-discipline
25. http://progressivevalues.org.s150046.gridserver.com/2013/05/page/3/
26. www.willpowered.co/learn/strengthen-your-willpower
27. www.bbc.com/news/magazine-16845204
28. http://advancedhabits.com/how-to-increase-willpower-exercising-your-brain/

29. www.century21.ca/varinder.puaar/Blog/The_One_
    Factor_That_Changes_Everything_By_Alex_Green
30. www.stickk.com

11 Persistence 115

1. www.brainyquote.com/quotes/quotes/c/calvin-
   cool414555.html
2. www.goodreads.com/quotes/26963-if-you-can-t-fly-
   then-run-if-you-can-t-run
3. https://books.google.ca/
   books?id=A709CQAAQBAJ&p-
   g=PA139&lpg=PA139&dq=Lack+of+persis-
   tence+is+one+of+the+major+causes+of+fail-
   ure.+Moreover,+experience+with+thousands+of+-
   people+has+proved+that+lack+of+persis-
   tence+is+a+weakness+common+to+the+majority-
   +of+men.+It+is+a+weakness+which+may+be+over-
   come+with+effort.%E2%80%9D&sour-
   ce=bl&ots=-nqaOW59tM&sig=I3gTNY-
   51wEJkIslQajoAffGp-4c&hl=en&sa=X&ei=W-
   wySVZuPF4W1-AHT04OwCQ&ved=0CC-
   gQ6AEwAw#v=onepage&q=Lack%20of%20
   persistence%20is%20one%20of%20the%20major%20
   causes%20of%20failure.%20Moreover%2C%20ex-
   perience%20with%20thousands%20of%20people%20
   has%20proved%20that%20lack%20of%20persist-
   ence%20is%20a%20weakness%20common%20to%20
   the%20majority%20of%20men.%20It%20is%20a%20
   weakness%20which%20may%20be%20overcome%20
   with%20effort.%E2%80%9D&f=false
4. www.inc.com/brent-gleeson/why-persistence-is-far-
   more-important-than-planning.html

5. www.businessinsider.co.id/successful-people-who-failed-at-first-2014-3/1/
6. www.positivelypositive.com/2013/06/12/big-failure-big-success-12-people-to-keep-you-going/
7. http://bambooinnovator.com/2014/02/27/steven-spielberg-got-rejected-from-film-school-three-times-oprah-winfrey-was-told-she-was-unfit-for-tv-stephen-king-received-30-rejections-for-carrie-w/
8. http://business.financialpost.com/business-insider/14-people-who-failed-before-becoming-super-successful-stars
9. http://genius.com/Napoleon-hill-think-and-grow-rich-chapter-9-annotated
10. http://michaelhyatt.com/developing-persistence.html
11. http://elusivelife.net/personal/self-improvement-personal/10-tips-to-develop-persistence
12. http://vnthomas1.blogspot.ca/2015/01/think-and-grow-rich-by-napoleon-hill.html
13. www.wikihow.com/Be-Persistent
14. www.wikihow.com/Be-Persistent
15. http://quickbase.intuit.com/blog/2011/07/26/the-dangers-of-setting-performance-goals/
16. www.excelatlife.com/articles/generalizing.htm
17. www.lifeoptimizer.org/2007/11/19/7-sure-fire-ways-to-develop-persistence/
18. www.essentiallifeskills.net/visualization.html
19. www.essentiallifeskills.net/overcoming-fear-of-failure.html

12 Happiness And Gratitude   133

1. www.huffingtonpost.com/belle-beth-cooper/10-simple-things-to-be-happy_b_4241824.html
2. www.huffingtonpost.com/belle-beth-cooper/10-simple-things-to-be-happy_b_4241824.html

3. www.huffingtonpost.com/belle-beth-cooper/10-simple-things-to-be-happy_b_4241824.html
4. www.huffingtonpost.com/belle-beth-cooper/10-simple-things-to-be-happy_b_4241824.html
5. www.inc.com/jeff-haden/10-scientifically-proven-ways-to-be-incredibly-happy-wed.html
6. https://blog.bufferapp.com/10-scientifically-proven-ways-to-make-yourself-happier
7. https://blog.bufferapp.com/10-scientifically-proven-ways-to-make-yourself-happier
8. www.psychologytoday.com/blog/the-athletes-way/201504/mindfulness-the-power-thinking-about-your-thinking
9. www.wsj.com/articles/SB10001424127887324144304578621951399427408
10. www.wikihow.com/Be-Happy
11. www.huffingtonpost.com/arianna-huffington/sleep-challenge-2010-slee_b_436341.html.
12. http://happsters.com/2013/10/24/5-ways-to-give-off-positive-energy/
13. http://en.wikipedia.org/wiki/Gratitude
14. www.wikihow.com/Build-Self-Confidence
15. "every day above ground is a great day" Pitbull
16. www.drchristinahibbert.com/10-ways-to-practice-gratitude-today/
17. "Gratitude is the heart's memory," www.everydayhealth.com/columns/therese-borchard-sanity-break/6-ways-to-cultivate-gratitude/
18. http://psychcentral.com/blog/archives/2013/12/28/6-ways-to-cultivate-gratitude/
19. www.drchristinahibbert.com/10-ways-to-practice-gratitude-today/

20. http://news.wustl.edu/news/Pages/20507.aspx
21. www.unstuck.com/gratitude.html

13 The Power Of Love   149

1. https://en.wikiquote.org/wiki/Sophocles
2. www.psychologytoday.com/blog/emotional-fitness/201405/what-love-gives-you
3. http://babiesneedmothers.com/articles/the-love-energy.html?start=2

14 Taking Care Of Your Body   155

1. http://ellinikahoaxes.gr/2014/08/16/nous-igiis/
2. www.lifehack.org/articles/productivity/7-monday-morning-habits-highly-successful-people.html
3. www.lifehack.org/articles/productivity/7-monday-morning-habits-highly-successful-people.html
4. www.livestrong.com/article/410524-how-does-exercise-help-the-brain/
5. www.livestrong.com/article/410524-how-does-exercise-help-the-brain/
6. www.livestrong.com/article/410524-how-does-exercise-help-the-brain/
7. www.livestrong.com/article/410524-how-does-exercise-help-the-brain/
8. www.livestrong.com/article/410524-how-does-exercise-help-the-brain/
9. www.breastcancer.org/tips/nutrition/healthy_eat
10. www.sharecare.com/health/water-liquid-nutrient/article/how-much-water-do-you-really-need
11. www.wikihow.com/Think-Positively

12. www.g4ed.com/stories/?p=697
13. www.health.harvard.edu/fhg/updates/update0606a.shtml

15 Take Action   161

1. https://en.wikiquote.org/wiki/Herodotus
2. www.quoteland.com/author/Napoleon-Hill-Quotes/641/
3. https://en.wikiquote.org/wiki/Napoleon_Hill
4. www.realsimple.com/work-life/life-strategies/inspiration-motivation/secrets-of-motivated-people/page2

16 Developing A Plan   167

1. www.brainyquote.com/quotes/quotes/n/napoleonhi389332.html
2. www.brainyquote.com/quotes/quotes/j/jimrohn165075.html
3. www.goodreads.com/quotes/87476-a-goal-without-a-plan-is-just-a-wish
4. Heidi Grant Halvorson, Columbia University professor http://jamesclear.com/implementation-intentions
5. John F. Kennedy. BrainyQuote.com, Xplore Inc, 2015. www.brainyquote.com/quotes/quotes/j/johnfkenn121068.html.

17 The Power Of ALL   179

1. www.brainyquote.com/quotes/quotes/n/napoleonhi385887.html

4. www.wikihow.com/Get-Motivated
5. https://en.wikipedia.org/wiki/B_vitamins
6. www.everydayhealth.com/diet-nutrition/benefits-of-vitamin-b6.aspx
7. www.mayoclinic.org/healthy-lifestyle/adult-health/in-depth/sleep/art-20048379
8. www.positivityblog.com/index.php/2007/06/13/25-simple-ways-to-motivate-yourself/
9. www.lifehack.org/articles/productivity/how-to-stay-motivated.html
10. www.forbes.com/sites/nextavenue/2013/07/19/how-to-stay-motivated-and-accomplish-anything/
11. www.positivityblog.com/index.php/2007/06/13/25-simple-ways-to-motivate-yourself/
12. www.excelatlife.com/articles/generalizing.htm
13. www.inc.com/geoffrey-james/10-thoughts-that-super-motivate-you.html
    http://omarperiu.com/#services
14. www.stevenaitchison.co.uk/blog/8-destructive-thinking-patterns-and-how-to-change-them/
15. http://brightdrops.com/best-motivational-quotes
16. www.positivityblog.com/index.php/2007/06/13/25-simple-ways-to-motivate-yourself/
17. www.lifehack.org/articles/productivity/thirteen-tricks-to-motivate-yourself.html
18. www.amazon.com/gp/product/0380810336?ie=UTF8&tag=sourcesofinsight-20&linkCode=as2&camp=1789&creative=9325&creativeASIN=0380810336
19. www.inc.com/rhett-power/1easy-tool-to-help-you-stay-focused-and-motivated.html
20. http://zenhabits.net/get-off-your-butt-16-ways-to-get-motivated-when-youre-in-a-slump/

21. http://sourcesofinsight.com/13-motivation-techniques/

21 Tools And Things To Do To Keep You Organized And Motivated   229

1. https://en.wikipedia.org/wiki/Mind_map
2. www.mindmeister.com/
3. http://zenhabits.net/27-great-tips-to-keep-your-life-organized/
4. http://zenhabits.net/27-great-tips-to-keep-your-life-organized/
5. www.lifehack.org/articles/productivity/7-monday-morning-habits-highly-successful-people.html
6. https://en.wikipedia.org/wiki/Pomodoro_Technique
7. http://management.about.com/cs/generalmanagement/a/Pareto081202.htm
8. www.asianefficiency.com/productivity/coveys-time-management-quadrant/
9. http://fatherhood.about.com/od/time-management-productivity/a/Stephen-Coveys-Four-Quadrants-And-Work-Life-Balance.htm
10. http://advancedlifeskills.com/blog/20-time-management-tips/
11. www.lifehack.org/articles/productivity/incredible-productivity-advice-given-21-successful-young-entrepreneurs.html
12. https://en.wikipedia.org/wiki/Imitation
13. macfreedom.com/
14. www.stickk.com

22 Mirroring And Imitating Successful People   247

1. www.forbes.com/sites/laurashin/2013/05/01/the-7-ways-successful-people-approach-their-work/
2. www.entrepreneur.com/article/237866
3. Tony Hsieh, Zappos http://dougsmanagementmoment.blogspot.ca/2012/07/4-reason-you-need-patienceright-now.html
4. www.lifehack.org/articles/productivity/this-how-you-can-develop-highly-successful-mind.html
5. www.businessinsider.com/how-successful-people-think-2015-4
6. www.linkedin.com/pulse/habits-set-ultra-successful-people-apart-dr-travis-bradberry
7. www.lifehack.org/articles/productivity/13-differences-between-successful-and-highly-successful-individuals.html
8. http://successify.net/2012/10/31/22-things-happy-people-do-differently/
9. www.lifehack.org/articles/productivity/8-differences-between-you-and-someone-who-successful.html
10. www.businessinsider.com/how-successful-people-think-john-maxwell-2011-9?op=1
11. www.lifehack.org/articles/featured/13-reasons-why-you-will-never-successful.html
12. www.lifehack.org/articles/communication/6-signs-that-you-are-already-successful.html

Other Resources:

- www.inc.com/geoffrey-james/how-to-motivate-yourself-14-easy-ways.html
- www.lifehack.org/articles/productivity/thirteen-tricks-to-motivate-yourself.html
- www.forbes.com/sites/glennllopis/2012/06/04/top-9-things-that-ultimately-motivate-employees-to-achieve/3/
- www.positivityblog.com/index.php/2007/06/13/25-simple-ways-to-motivate-yourself/
- http://sourcesofinsight.com/13-motivation-techniques/
- http://jamesclear.com/implementation-intentions